CARYL CHURCHILL

Caryl Churchill has written for the stage, television and radio. Her stage plays include *Owners* (Royal Court Theatre Upstairs, 1972); *Objections to Sex and Violence* (Royal Court, 1975), *Light Shining in Buckinghamshire* (Joint Stock on tour incl. Theatre Upstairs, 1976); *Vinegar Tom* (Monstrous Regiment on tour, incl. Half Moon and ICA, 1976); *Traps* (Theatre Upstairs , 1977); *Cloud Nine* (Joint Stock on tour incl. Royal Court, London, 1979, then Theatre de Lys, New York, 1981); *Three More Sleepless Nights* (Soho Poly and Theatre Upstairs, 1980); *Top Girls* (Royal Court London, then Public Theater, New York, 1982); *Fen* (Joint Stock on tour, incl. Almeida and Royal Court, London, then Public Theater, New York, 1983); *Softcops* (RSC at the Pit, 1984); *A Mouthful of Birds* with David Lan (Joint Stock on tour, incl. Royal Court, 1986); *Serious Money* (Royal Court and Wyndham's, London, then Public Theater, New York, 1987); *Icecream* (Royal Court, 1989); *Mad Forest* (Central School of Speech and Drama, then Royal Court, 1990); *Lives of the Great Poisoners* with Orlando Gough and Ian Spink (Second Stride on tour, incl. Riverside Studios, London, 1991); *The Skriker* (Royal National Theatre, 1994); *Thyestes* translated from Seneca (Royal Court Theatre Upstairs, 1994); *Hotel* with Orlando Gough and Ian Spink (Second Stride on tour, incl. The Place, London, 1997); *This is a Chair* (London International Festival of Theatre at the Royal Court, 1997); *Blue Heart* (Joint Stock on tour, incl. Royal Court Theatre, 1997); *Far Away* (Royal Court Theatre Upstairs, 2000, and Albery, London, 2001, then New York Theatre Workshop, 2002); *A Number* (Royal Court Theatre Downstairs, 2002, then New York Theatre Workshop, 2004); *A Dream Play* after Strindberg (Royal National Theatre, 2005); *Drunk Enough to Say I Love You?* (Royal Court Theatre Downstairs, 2006, then Public Theater, New York, 2008); *Bliss* translated from Olivier Choinière (Royal Court Theatre Upstairs, 2008); *Seven Jewish Children – a play for Gaza* (Royal Court Theatre Downstairs, 2009); *Love and Information* (Royal Court Theatre Downstairs, 2012); *Ding Dong the Wicked* (Royal Court Theatre Downstairs, 2012); *Here We Go* (National Theatre, 2015); *Escaped Alone* (Royal Court Theatre Downstairs, 2016); *Pigs and Dogs* (Royal Court Theatre Downstairs, 2016).

CARYL CHURCHILL
Plays: Five

introduced by the author

Seven Jewish Children
Love and Information
Ding Dong the Wicked
Here We Go
Escaped Alone
Pigs and Dogs
War and Peace Gaza Piece
Tickets are Now On Sale
Beautiful Eyes

NICK HERN BOOKS
London

www.nickhernbooks.co.uk

A Nick Hern Book

Churchill Plays: Five first published in Great Britain as a paperback
original in 2019 by Nick Hern Books Limited, The Glasshouse,
49a Goldhawk Road, London W12 8QP

Author photograph: Marc Brenner

Designed and typeset by Nick Hern Books
Printed in Great Britain by Mimeo Ltd, Huntingdon, Cambridgeshire
PE29 6XX

ISBN 978 1 84842 824 9

Contents

Introduction

Some of these plays were written quickly, triggered by specific events, others not. *Love and Information* has the longest background, starting as a few scenes in the 90s which I abandoned, and rediscovered fifteen years later. I kept a few of the original scenes – 'Virtual' is one – and this time saw what I wanted to do and wrote the rest. By contrast, I wrote *Seven Jewish Children* in January 2009 at the time of Israel's bombing of Gaza in which over 1000 people were killed. Dominic Cooke at the Royal Court responded at once and it was on stage in early February and online soon after.

The three other very short plays were written in response to being asked. In 2014 Jonathan Chadwick of Az Theatre, which has a relationship with Theatre for Everybody in Gaza, wanted contributions to an evening launching a cooperative project based on Tolstoy's *War and Peace*. He suggested looking at a short section of the novel, and I had also read accounts by one of his colleagues in Gaza of family life there. *War and Peace Gaza Piece* came from that. The following year Cressida Brown of Offstage Theatre produced a show of short plays, *Walking the Tightrope: the tension between art and politics*. I'd been concerned for some time about the complicated issue of sponsorship, and the implications for the arts of being used as part of an advertising campaign to boost the image of a product. Fossil-fuel firms are particularly keen to look attractive, and I knew about the spectacular disruptions by the activist group 'BP or Not BP' at the RSC and the British Museum. In 2017, the week of Trump's inauguration, Cressida put on a show called *Top Trumps* and my piece for that was *Beautiful Eyes*.

Pigs and Dogs was less immediately topical, but it did come from news of a surge in action against homosexuality in Uganda, where the death penalty was proposed though later withdrawn, and from reading the book *Boy-Wives and Female Husband*s, a collection of material edited by Stephen O. Murray and Will Roscoe showing how varied and fluid sexuality was in many African tribes before European Christian missionaries imposed rigidity and intolerance. Many former colonies have taken those laws and values on board and come to regard them as their own, seeing recent Western acceptance of homosexuality as a colonial imposition and, ironically, welcoming American missionaries who condemn it.

The other plays, like *Love and Information*, have less clear origins, though *Ding Dong the Wicked* suddenly became possible when I had the idea of making two families on separate sides in a war use exactly the same words. I think I've been accurate down to the 'and's and 'the's, not that anyone seeing or reading the play would know. I can't think of anything to tell about *Here We Go*, except an old person having said to me how boring it became that trivial things like getting washed and dressed now took up so much time. There was more to it than that of course, as there was more to *Escaped Alone* than once seeing some women in a back yard through an open gate in a fence.

C.C.

SEVEN JEWISH CHILDREN

a play for Gaza

Seven Jewish Children was first performed at the Royal Court
Theatre Downstairs, London, on 6 February 2009. The cast was
as follows:

Ben Caplin
Jack Chissick
David Horovitch
Daisy Lewis
Ruth Posner
Samuel Roukin
Jennie Stoller
Susannah Wise
Alexis Zegerman

Director	Dominic Cooke
Lighting Designer	Jack Williams
Sound Designer	Alexander Caplan

The play can be read or performed anywhere, by any number
of people. Anyone who wishes to do it should contact the
author's agent (see details on page iv), who will license
performances free of charge provided that no admission fee is
charged and that a collection is taken at each performance for
Medical Aid for Palestinians (MAP), www.map-uk.org

Note

No children appear in the play. The speakers are adults, the parents and if you like other relations of the children. The lines can be shared out in any way you like among those characters. The characters are different in each small scene as the time and child are different. They may be played by any number of actors.

The play starts during a nineteenth-century Russian pogrom and ends during the bombing of Gaza in 2009.

1.

Tell her it's a game

Tell her it's serious

But don't frighten her

Don't tell her they'll kill her

Tell her it's important to be quiet

Tell her she'll have cake if she's good

Tell her to curl up as if she's in bed

But not to sing.

Tell her not to come out

Tell her not to come out even if she hears shouting

Don't frighten her

Tell her not to come out even if she hears nothing for a long
time

Tell her we'll come and find her

Tell her we'll be here all the time.

Tell her something about the men

Tell her they're bad in the game

Tell her it's a story

Tell her they'll go away

Tell her she can make them go away if she keeps still

By magic

But not to sing.

2.

Tell her this is a photograph of her grandmother, her uncles and me

Tell her her uncles died

Don't tell her they were killed

Tell her they were killed

Don't frighten her.

Tell her her grandmother was clever

Don't tell her what they did

Tell her she was brave

Tell her she taught me how to make cakes

Don't tell her what they did

Tell her something

Tell her more when she's older.

Tell her there were people who hated Jews

Don't tell her

Tell her it's over now

Tell her there are still people who hate Jews

Tell her there are people who love Jews

Don't tell her to think Jews or not Jews

Tell her more when she's older

Tell her how many when she's older

Tell her it was before she was born and she's not in danger

Don't tell her there's any question of danger.

Tell her we love her

Tell her dead or alive her family all love her

Tell her her grandmother would be proud of her.

3.

Don't tell her we're going for ever

Tell her she can write to her friends, tell her her friends can maybe come and visit

Tell her it's sunny there

Tell her we're going home

Tell her it's the land God gave us

Don't tell her religion

Tell her her great great great great lots of greats grandad lived there

Don't tell her he was driven out

Tell her, of course tell her, tell her everyone was driven out and the country is waiting for us to come home

Don't tell her she doesn't belong here

Tell her of course she likes it here but she'll like it there even more.

Tell her it's an adventure

Tell her no one will tease her

Tell her she'll have new friends

Tell her she can take her toys

Don't tell her she can take all her toys

Tell her she's a special girl

Tell her about Jerusalem.

4.

Don't tell her who they are

Tell her something

Tell her they're Bedouin, they travel about

Tell her about camels in the desert and dates

Tell her they live in tents

Tell her this wasn't their home

Don't tell her home, not home, tell her they're going away

Don't tell her they don't like her

Tell her to be careful.

Don't tell her who used to live in this house

No but don't tell her her great great grandfather used to live in this house

No but don't tell her Arabs used to sleep in her bedroom.

Tell her not to be rude to them

Tell her not to be frightened

Tell her they're good people and they work for us.

Don't tell her she can't play with the children

Don't tell her she can have them in the house.

Tell her they have plenty of friends and family

Tell her for miles and miles all round they have lands of their own

Tell her again this is our promised land.

Don't tell her they said it was a land without people

Don't tell her I wouldn't have come if I'd known.

Tell her maybe we can share.

Don't tell her that.

5.

Tell her we won

Tell her her brother's a hero

Tell her how big their armies are

Tell her we turned them back

Tell her we're fighters

Tell her we've got new land.

6.

Don't tell her

Don't tell her the trouble about the swimming pool

Tell her it's our water, we have the right

Tell her it's not the water for their fields

Don't tell her anything about water.

Don't tell her about the bulldozer

Don't tell her not to look at the bulldozer

Don't tell her it was knocking the house down

Tell her it's a building site

Don't tell her anything about bulldozers.

Don't tell her about the queues at the checkpoint

Tell her we'll be there in no time

Don't tell her anything she doesn't ask

Don't tell her the boy was shot

Don't tell her anything.

Tell her we're making new farms in the desert

Don't tell her about the olive trees

Tell her we're building new towns in the wilderness.

Don't tell her they throw stones

Tell her they're not much good against tanks

Don't tell her that.

Don't tell her they set off bombs in cafés

Tell her, tell her they set off bombs in cafés

Tell her to be careful

Don't frighten her.

Tell her we need the wall to keep us safe

Tell her they want to drive us into the sea

Tell her they don't

Tell her they want to drive us into the sea.

Tell her we kill far more of them

Don't tell her that

Tell her that

Tell her we're stronger

Tell her we're entitled

Tell her they don't understand anything except violence

Tell her we want peace

Tell her we're going swimming.

7.

Tell her she can't watch the news

Tell her she can watch cartoons

Tell her she can stay up late and watch Friends.

Tell her they're attacking with rockets

Don't frighten her

Tell her only a few of us have been killed

Tell her the army has come to our defence

Don't tell her her cousin refused to serve in the army.

Don't tell her how many of them have been killed

Tell her the Hamas fighters have been killed

Tell her they're terrorists

Tell her they're filth

Don't

Don't tell her about the family of dead girls

Tell her you can't believe what you see on television

Tell her we killed the babies by mistake

Don't tell her anything about the army

Tell her, tell her about the army, tell her to be proud of the army. Tell her about the family of dead girls, tell her their names why not, tell her the whole world knows why shouldn't she know? tell her there's dead babies, did she see babies? tell her she's got nothing to be ashamed of. Tell her they did it to themselves. Tell her they want their children killed to make people sorry for them, tell her I'm not sorry for them, tell her not to be sorry for them, tell her we're the ones to be sorry for, tell her they can't talk suffering to us. Tell her we're the iron fist now, tell her it's the fog of war, tell her we won't stop killing them till we're safe, tell her I laughed when I saw the dead policemen, tell her they're animals living in rubble now, tell her I wouldn't care if we wiped them out, the world would hate us is the only thing, tell her I don't care if the world hates us, tell her we're better haters, tell her we're chosen people, tell her I look at one of their children covered in blood and what do I feel? tell her all I feel is happy it's not her.

Don't tell her that.

Tell her we love her.

Don't frighten her.

LOVE AND INFORMATION

Love and Information was first performed at the Royal Court Theatre Downstairs, London, on 6 September 2012. The cast was as follows:

Nikki Amuka-Bird
Linda Bassett
Scarlett Brookes
Amanda Drew
Susan Engel
Laura Elphinstone
John Heffernan
Joshua James
Paul Jesson
Billy Matthews
Justin Salinger
Amit Shah
Rhashan Stone
Nell Williams
Josh Williams
Sarah Woodward

Director	James Macdonald
Set Designer	Miriam Buether
Costume Designer	Laura Hopkins
Lighting Designer	Peter Mumford
Sound Designer	Christopher Shutt

Note

The sections should be played in the order given but the scenes can be played in any order within each section.

There are random scenes, see at the end, which can happen any time. They need not be included, except Depression, which is an essential part of the play.

The characters are different in every scene. The only possible exception to this are the random Depression scenes, which could be the same two people, or the same depressed person with different others. In Piano, the singer can be a man – just change the name. I'm indicating with numbers the speakers in Piano because there's been confusion in some productions about what's happening.

Caryl Churchill gratefully acknowledges that the LAB scene is based on material from *The Making of Memory* by Steven Rose, published by Bantam in 1992, revised edition published by Viking in 2003.

1

SECRET

Please please tell me

no

please because I'll never

don't ask don't ask

I'll never tell

no

no matter what

it's not

I'd die before I told

it's not you telling, even if you didn't

I wouldn't

it's you knowing it's too awful I can't

but tell me

no

because if you don't there's this secret between us

stop it

if there's this secret we're not

please

we're not close any more we can't ever

but nobody knows everything about

yes but a big secret like this

it's not such a big

then tell me

will you stop

it's big because you won't tell me

no I won't.

Is it something you've

don't start guessing

or something you want to

please

or you've seen or heard or know or

please

and if it's something you've done is it a crime or a sin or just
embarrassing because whichever

no I don't want you to know.

All right.

All right I'll tell you

you don't have to

I'll tell you

yes tell me because I'll never

it's not that

tell me because I'll always

all right I'm telling you.

Tells in a whisper.

No

yes

no

I warned you

but that's

yes

oh no that's

yes

how could you

I did.

Now what? now what? now what?

CENSUS

Why do they need to know all this stuff?

They're doing research. It guides their policy. They use it to help people.

They use it to sell us things we don't want.

No that's the people who phone up. I don't answer any of their questions, I just say No thank you, there's no need to swear at them.

I've made a mess of it now anyway.

You'll get into trouble if you don't do it.

They won't know.

They know you exist.

FAN

Love him so much

love him more than you

I'd jump out of the window

eat fire

cut off my hand

eat dogshit

kill my mother

eat catfood

yeuch

just to touch him

just to tell him

just to see him

just to have him see me.

He was born at ten past two in the morning and I was born at two past ten

how do you know?

Mum says

two past ten

she said just after ten so that's two

that isn't two

it is two

anyway he was born on Tuesday and I was born on Wednesday and you were only born on Friday

that's stupid.

His favourite colour's blue

favourite food's chilli

favourite animal's snakes

favourite holiday was in Bermuda

what's his favourite smell?

Roses

you're making that up

well what?

I'm asking you

you don't know

I'm asking you

you don't know do you go on tell me

you tell me

I don't know you tell me

all right I don't know so we've got to find out

you mean neither of us know?

It's all right we'll find out

I can't believe neither of us

it's in here somewhere

I know I used to know

wait

is it chicken?

wait

you can't find it

I can't

you're not looking properly

I can't find it

here let me

you can't find it

wait

it's not there

wait

see you can't.

What are we going to do?

we've got to know

I won't be able to sleep

what are we going to do?

TORTURE

He's wearing me out.

Take a break.

Do you want to go in?

I'll give him a cigarette.

He's not ready to talk.

I thought we'd got there yesterday.

I thought we'd got there yesterday but he's past that.

He'll get to where he'll say anything.

We're not paid extra for it to be true.

I'll give him a cigarette while you have a cigarette and I'll tell him you'll be back.

LAB

So we hatch a batch of eggs in the lab

and where do you get the

from the poultry breeders who supply them to the battery

oh the intensive

yes or some of them might go to farms but either way

so either way they're going to be

yes by twelve weeks they'll be plucked and lying on their backs in a supermarket

on your table

so you're not taking the life

I am taking the life

but even if you didn't they'd be

they wouldn't live to be old chickens, no.

So you've got the chickens and

about a day old, fluffy yellow like little Easter

and you do some experiment on them?

what we do is we get them to peck

because chicks do peck a lot

they peck at everything and what we do is we get them to peck beads that have been dipped either in water or some stuff that tastes bitter

not poison

no it makes them wipe their beaks on the floor then they're fine again and of course we're writing all this down which chick which bead and how many pecks and then my colleague injects this tiny amount of very slightly radioactive liquid into each side of the chick's brain so

oh no stop

I know but they don't seem at all

it doesn't hurt

they don't show any

ok so what's it for? it's going to show up something in their brains

because what we've injected has a sugar in it that gets used by the nerve cells and the more sugar is taken up the more brain activity and the radioactivity acts as a tracer like in a scanner so you can measure that and see exactly where in the brain the sugar

and the idea is it's different in the different

what we hope to see you see is that it's different

depending on what they've learned about the

yes because we give them the beads again and they have learned
because the ones who had the beads with water come back and
peck it again and the ones

they won't peck it

the ones that had the bitter bead have learned not to peck it

that's terrific.

But that's not what we're finding out, what we're finding out

changes in the brain

exactly, what changes in the brain correspond to that memory

so to do that you have to

yes I hold the bird in my left hand and quickly cut off its head
with a big pair of scissors

aah

and I drop the body in a bucket and take the head and peel
back the skin and cut round the skull and there's the brain

there's the brain

so I put it in a dish of ice and my colleague cuts it into slabs
with a razor blade and then he dissects out tiny samples that he
puts into test tubes and they're immediately frozen while
meanwhile I'm taking the brain out of the next chick

yes

and that's what I do.

And then you analyse

yes and there is a substantial increase

so you can measure

and not just the increase but exactly where because if you slice

slice the brain

slice the frozen brain into thin sections and put them on slides you get pictures

you can see

you can see exactly depending on how dark and you can convert it into false colour which of course looks

prettier

prettier yes and easier to read though the information is the same

which is

that the learning takes place on the left side of the brain

and you can see

and there's another version where you stain the sample with silver salts and then you can count the new spines on the dendrites which are

yes the little tiny

because at that degree of magnification a thumbnail would be two hundred and fifty metres wide

so you can see the memory

yes you can see the actual changes

see what the chick learnt about the bead.

SLEEP

I can't sleep.

Hot milk.

I hate it now.

Book?

I haven't got one I like.

Just lie there and breathe.

My head's too full of stuff. Are you asleep?

No no, what, it's fine. You can't sleep?

I think I'll get up and go on Facebook.

REMOTE

You don't seem to have a tv.

There used to be one but it stopped working. The reception's no good anyhow.

I brought my laptop.

You might have a reception problem there.

It's not that I need it. There's no phone signal is there?

You'd have to go to town. Or I think someone said there's a spot about two miles up the road if you go down towards the cliff and stand on a rock, you'd have to know it.

We can listen to the radio. Does it work?

I did warn you.

I know.

It's quiet here.

I like it quiet.

You can always cycle down and get a newspaper.

It's all right.

I don't have time you see.

Don't you sometimes want a weather forecast?

I want you to be happy here.

I am happy here.

You'll find you can feel if it's raining.

2

IRRATIONAL

Is an irrational number real?

It's real to me.

But can you have an irrational number of oranges?

Not as things stand, no.

I'm not comfortable with the whole idea.

There was someone called Hippasus in Greek times who found out about the diagonal of a square and they drowned him because no one wanted to know about things like that.

Like what?

Numbers that make you uncomfortable and don't relate to oranges.

I can see how they might want to do that.

Drown him?

Maybe he should have kept quiet about it if he knew they couldn't stand it.

Is that what you do?

AFFAIR

I don't know if I should tell you.

What?

But you're my friend more than she is.

What is it?

What do you think yourself? is it better to know things or not to know things? Is it better just to let things be the way you think they are, the way they are really because if someone tells you something that might change everything and do you want that? Do you think it's interfering or is it what a friend ought to do?

You're going to have to tell me now, you know that.

But some people might say you shouldn't say anything because you might not want to hear anything against your best friend but I do keep seeing them together and last night I was having a drink with her after work and he just sort of turned up and after a bit they left together, they hardly bothered to come up with a story, I just wondered. I'm probably imagining things and I shouldn't put ideas into your head because it may all be perfectly all right, I'm sorry maybe I should have kept quiet, oh dear, I've told you now.

They're having an affair.

They are? you know that? you knew that?

I've known that quite a while.

How long?

Three years.

And you're ok with it?

Yes it's all ok. Thanks though.

MOTHER

While Mum's out

what?

I've something to tell you

ok

so you need to look at me

I'm listening

I need to feel you're really paying attention

I can pay attention and do other things at the same time, I'm not brain-dead, I can see and hear and everything

will you listen?

I'm listening, fuck off. Is this going to take long?

Don't pay attention then, I'm just telling you, you might like to know Mum's not your mother, I'm your mother, Mum's your nan, ok? Did you listen to that?

Does Mum know you're telling me?

I just decided.

Are we going to tell her you told me?

I don't know. Do you think?

Why didn't she say before, she doesn't want me to know, she's going to go crazy

it'll be ok

it's not my fault, she can't blame me for knowing

it'll be ok, I'll tell her I told you, it's my fault.

How old were you, wait, thirteen. You were thirteen? Thirteen.

Yes, that's why.

It's probably better than not being born.

That's what I thought, I thought you'd like to be born.

Who's my dad then?

I didn't see him any more, he went to a different school. He was twelve.

I don't think I feel like you're my mum though. I don't have a sister, I don't like that. Do you want me to feel different about you?

I just didn't want it to be something I could never say.

I'd like it if everything could go on like it was.

You mean not tell Mum?

Do we have to?

But then you'd have something you could never say.

I've got a stomach ache.

I don't care if she goes crazy.

So long as it's you she goes crazy with.

I can tell her to leave you alone because I'm your mum.

I don't think that works.

FIRED

You shouldn't fire people by email.

You can't come bursting in here and shouting.

I'm just saying it needs to be face to face.

I'm sorry, I do appreciate, but I'm busy at the moment, if you could

I need to be looked in the eye and you say you're firing me

redundancy isn't

just say it to my face, you're fired, just say it, you're a coward you can't say it

why don't you speak to my p.a. and make an appointment

just say it, you're fired, just say it

MESSAGE

It's a message

killing people

yes because then they understand

killing yourself

they understand what you're telling them

but they don't do they, they just

because the deaths show how important it is

no they just say you're a terrorist or

and the terror is a message

but they don't get it do they, they just pass laws and lock people up and

if enough people did it because they don't really feel terror do they, they don't live in terror, if they lived in terror they'd be getting the message.

Would you do it yourself?

I don't think I would, no.

Because you're scared?

I don't think that message is what I want to say.

GRASS

What did you do that for?

I thought

What do you think's going to happen to you?

I know but

and to me and the children did you think about that?

It seemed like the right thing to do.

So will we have to change who we are and go and live somewhere else?

I didn't say

and you'll be a protected witness and all our life we'll be living in fear in a mobile home in a desert in America?

I didn't say who I was, I just made the phone call

from your own phone?

no of course not from my own phone, I'm not stupid

well you are but ok, from a public

yes of course

but near here like in the high street

no I took a train

you took a train? when?

today, to make the call, I went to Brighton

why Brighton?

I don't know, it's somewhere you can go quickly on a train

so you didn't go to work? You weren't at work you could've got the kids from school

I was in Brighton

I'd have liked a day out in Brighton

it wasn't a day out in Brighton, I made the call on a public phone in Brighton, I had a coffee and I got the train back.

And what did you say?

I just gave them the name, I said this is the person you want in connection with, no I won't give my name thank you, goodbye. That's all.

But if they know the call came from Brighton and they could find out who knew him who went to Brighton

they won't do that, they don't need to know who I am, they just need to know who to look at but if he finds out you went to Brighton

but he's not going to know what I did in Brighton

you can't be sure of that, what if he's got a mate in the police who says we got a tip it was you, it came from Brighton, and someone else tells him they saw you get on a train to go to Brighton

how likely is that? why would he have a mate in the police? of course he doesn't have a mate in the police, do I have a mate in the police, you're making a whole thing up that's not going to happen.

I don't see why you had to do it.

It wasn't very nice what he did, was it.

He's a friend of yours.

He's not a friend of mine.

He's not now. He doesn't know he's not now, what if you see him? what if I see him? what if he comes round here and says the police are on to me what am I going to do can you help me?

You're making things up again.

No I'm not. That's what's going to happen.

TERMINAL

Doctor, one thing before I go. Can you tell me how long I've got?

There's not an exact answer to that.

I'd be grateful for anything you can give me an idea.

Well let me say ten per cent of people with this condition are still alive after three years.

That's helpful, thank you.

3

SCHIZOPHRENIC

How do you know I'm evil?

I've been told it.

Who by? Who by?

You know the traffic lights at the corner?

yes

I'm getting signals. The ones on the left as you go up from here.

Ok and what do they say?

I won't tell you.

Why not?

Because it's about you, it's what you're like, and you know that yourself I'm not going to say it.

Do they tell you to hurt people?

Not people. You.

But you know when you take your medication that doesn't happen.

That's why I stopped because it was making it hard to get the information.

You do know you're ill.

I've been told that.

SPIES

So we went to war on a completely

yes but how were they to know

they did know, they knew, he'd already admitted it wasn't true

he said it to the Germans

and the CIA knew

but Bush and Blair didn't know

didn't want to know

they had to rely

they wanted it to be true

they thought it was true, everyone thought

not everyone no, plenty of people, I didn't, I always knew it wasn't true

you can't have known

I knew it was all made-up stuff

and how did you know?

because of what America's like, what it wanted to do

you didn't know it was made up, you wanted it to be made up, that's what you wanted to be true.

And it turns out I was right, didn't it.

Do you think you've just won an argument?

DREAM

I had this dream last night, I was in a garden and there were blackberries, big bushes of brambles, I was picking them, and a butterfly flew across and I could see this orange-and-black butterfly really clearly on a yellow rose, but then the whole thing was a dance because I was at the ballet. And I looked all those things up on a website about dreams, blackberry, butterfly, ballet, and every single one means infidelity. So now I know he's cheating.

So you don't feel you have to be faithful to him any more?

No, why should I?

So that leaves the way clear for us?

Don't you think?

Unless it's not about him.

Who then?

You. You and me.

That would mean we're definitely going to do it.

So either way.

Either way.

RECLUSE

Two inside, one outside the door who can be heard.

Don't answer

it's only

look through the spyhole.

You're right, I thought it was the boy delivering the

don't answer don't

of course I won't answer, don't panic.

Hello. Hello Mr Rushmore. I believe this is where you live. We saw you going in, we know the car outside is

make him go away

shall I speak to him?

yes no no

and of course I respect your desire for privacy and it would so much help your thousands of admirers to understand if you could say a few words to us about that privacy about how it feels to live here in a forest miles from

I'm going to die

sh it's all right

five minutes of your time I could explain to the world why you've chosen to leave it all behind and withdraw to this remote

I should have a gun

because that would enable you to set the record straight about your ex-wife's allegations of

I'm going to bed

to confirm or deny that you said of the Queen that she

I'll have to hide in the cupboard

to put an end to speculation once and for all about your

I'd kill myself but they'd write an obituary

shall I tell him to

no no because then they'll write about you

it doesn't matter

it does they mustn't if they know about you if you talk to them I'll never see you again

because we have a photograph of you taken last week in the

why don't I just

ALL RIGHT.

What?

Hello, Mr Rushmore?

I have three things to say. I am now a citizen of China. I have six illegitimate children. I have recently been abducted by aliens and returned to earth unharmed.

Mr Rushmore, if you could just open the door for a moment

that's all right you see that's fine if I tell him lies that's fine I haven't told them anything about myself at all that's fine I feel fine about that I think that's fine I think I feel fine about

and when exactly were you last in China?

that's fine that's fine

good good I'm glad you feel ok about

and will he go away now?

in a while he's sure to go away in a while if we keep

Mr Rushmore

Time passes.

He's gone.

He's gone.

Well that's all right then

yes

you handled that very

no I feel

what?

I feel terrible I feel

but you didn't tell him

but he knows

he doesn't know anything it was lies

he knows I'm the person that told those lies

no because he doesn't know it was lies

yes but he knows I said

you mean he'll work out it's lies and

whichever whichever he knows I said those words he knows I was in this room we'll have to move he knows it was me he knows I shouted out those

so you don't feel as good as you

no no I don't I feel

GOD'S VOICE

God told you to do it?

He did, yes.

How?

How do you mean, how?

Did you hear words?

It was the word of God.

But like something you could hear with your ears, actual words
from outside you?

They came into me.

The words.

What God said.

So you didn't exactly hear…?

In my heart.

So how does that work then?

I was praying about it

in words?

sometimes in words, sometimes just

silently

the words were silent, I was praying in

in your head

if you like, my head my heart

so sometimes in words and sometimes

sometimes just being in a state where I was praying

I don't know what state that is

well you'll have to take it from me there is such a state

ok, so there you are praying

praying and not knowing, seeking guidance, open to guidance from God

ok

and he told me what to do.

What's his voice like?

Firm. Kind.

He speaks English?

What sort of a question is that?

I know but does he speak rp or have a regional accent? I'm trying to understand what you heard.

It wasn't hearing like I hear you but it was hearing.

And he definitely said do it.

He said do it.

In words.

In words and inside me in knowing it was the right thing to do.

In your heart?

Right through my whole being.

In your toes?

Yes in my toes, will you stop now?

THE CHILD WHO DIDN'T KNOW FEAR

One person tells a story to another.

Once upon a time there was a child who didn't know what fear was and he wanted to find out. So his friends said, Cold shiver down your back, legs go funny, sometimes your hands no not your hands yes your hands tingle, it's more in your head, it's in your stomach, your belly you shit yourself, you can't breathe, your skin your skin creeps, it's a shiver a shudder do you really not know what it is? And the child said, I don't know what you mean. So they took him to a big dark empty house everyone said was haunted. They said, No one's ever been able to stay here till morning, you won't stay till midnight, you won't last a hour, and the child said, Why, what's going to happen? And they said, You'll know what we mean about being frightened. And the child said, Good, that's what I want to know. So in the morning his friends came back and there was the child sitting in the dusty room. And they said, You're still here? what happened? And the child said, There were things walking about, dead things, some of them didn't have heads and a monster with glowing – and his friends said, Didn't you run away? and the child said, There were weird noises like screams and like music but not music, and his friends said, What did you feel? and the child said, It came right up to me and put out its hand, and his friends said, Didn't your hair your stomach the back of your neck your legs weren't you frightened? And the child said, No, it's no good, I didn't feel anything, I still don't know what fear is. And on the way home he met a lion and the lion ate him.

STAR

It takes the light two point eight million years to get here.

So we're looking at two point eight million years ago.

It might not be there. It could have died by now.

So who's going to see that?

It might not even be people by then. The sun's only eight minutes.

In the morning let's wait eight minutes and see if it's there now.

4

WEDDING VIDEO

Several people.

This is the bit

this is the funny bit watch

where he spills

ah ah ha ha ha

gets me every time

and look look the sweet

and wasn't she little then

just a tiny girl in her pink

and now she's my god you should see

and her boyfriend

have you met him he's the most

and there's that woman

we never knew who she was

yes she's there in the video but who invited

someone who just goes to strangers' weddings

there she is talking to who is that that uncle of yours is it no

and look at the dresses I mean

because now you wouldn't dream

it shows you it's history

yes the children like it because

and the grandchildren are going to

and it can go down in the family and they can see

and all the ones of them as babies and little

and all the ones of their weddings and their

but it's sad we haven't got our grandparents' wedding video

or great great

or everybody that ever lived videos of

Henry the Eighth

Jesus walking on the

no further back if we had cave if we had Neanderthal

and dinosaurs

but who'd be working the camera?

and things coming out of the sea and tiny specks

then we'd know we'd know

we could keep

we'd know what

because I wouldn't remember all this if without the video I
wouldn't remember hardly anything at all about it because I
can't remember anything about that day that's not on the video
not clearly

I can remember putting the ring

no I can't see that in my mind's

and someone was sick

oh look it's the speeches now listen to Dad's speech it's so

SAVANT

What did you have for lunch on October the third 1998?

Chicken soup and a salad. I was at home. I had the chicken soup in a blue bowl. The salad had tomatoes, lettuce and chicory but no onion because I didn't want my breath to smell of onion when I went to the movies with my brother in the afternoon. The movie began at 2.15.

What was the movie?

Godzilla.

What happened in it?

You want the whole thing? Shot by shot?

Can you do that?

Let's not do that.

Ok. I remember Godzilla. There's a lizard that's been irradiated by a nuclear explosion so it's a monster and it goes to New York and the American military drops bombs on it.

That's the one.

What did you do afterwards?

We walked back to my brother's place and had poached eggs on toast. I had two cups of tea in his red mug, the one with a chip.

What was the weather like?

Rain in the morning but it cleared up. Rain in the evening. Rain the next morning.

June the sixth 2004.

EX

I'm glad we've done it, just to see

so am I

after all these years

because it was very important at the time, it's been very important

it has for me, all my life, very important

so never to have seen each other again would have been

it would have been impossible

it would have been sad anyway.

You remember the Italian restaurant?

no, yes, on the corner was it?

with the bushes outside?

no, I'm mixing it up with

I can see the waiter now

no, I can't get the waiter

the waiter with the moustache who always smiled so much when we came in.

I used to have spaghetti carbonara and you had vongole.

I can't remember eating, no, I was too busy looking at you probably.

I really loved you then.

I loved you.

I always remember you standing in that field

I wonder where that was, was it

all the buttercups.

I've got a really clear picture of you running ahead of me down a street. We were running for a bus I think.

Do you remember that hotel, we took a room for a couple of hours in a hotel, there was green wallpaper and we stood there kissing.

I remember the first time

no, that's got overlaid by so many other times, I can't, I remember once by a river, we were practically on a public footpath

the kitchen, the kitchen at your friend's house

which friend?

I never knew your friends' names

was it Chris? Terry?

I don't know, you remember the kitchen?

I might if I knew which house. Did we do it in a kitchen?

Behind the door. There was soup on the cooker.

I remember us just looking at each other.

The time in the street, we just stopped.

I was thinking more a time when you were sitting on the side of the bed.

Was that early on or near the end?

Near the end I think. Do you know the time I mean?

I sometimes go past that coffee shop.

Which one?

The one where we kept trying to say goodbye.

I think I've blotted that whole day out.

We were really happy.

Or sad, we used to cry.

Did we?

Sometimes.

MEMORY HOUSE

to improve my mind

no but you've got a good

my memory to improve

forget a lot?

not not

like names

like names like faces

we all

yes but

not worth worrying

but I've got to learn

ah

huge amount of memorising

of course

vocabulary

yes

statistics

statistics

every imaginable

I see your point

stacks of information which I have to

somehow

somehow acquire and retain.

So how do you intend

this course this memory

to improve your

lists lists as exercises

like getting the muscles

muscles of the brain

which of course I know it doesn't have muscles

and more than that a technique

for remembering

ancient ancient technique Romans

didn't know they

and all sorts Renaissance

they had a lot of brains then in the

Leonardo da Vinci

so did he?

I don't know that he actually did

not this technique

not necessarily this actual technique

though he might have done

it's beside the point, the point

the actual technique

the actual technique is you take a place like you could take a house

take a house?

in your mind this is a mental take a house you know in your mind

like my aunt's got a house

there you are take this house in your mind and you've got a list of things you want to remember

like what?

like anything like this list I've got here this exercise

crocodile pincushion

and you go round the house in your mind you go round and you put something in each room

can't quite remember all the rooms because

can't remember the rooms?

in my aunt's house I've never

take where you live

only be able to remember three things

no you could go round the room and put one on the table and one on the chair

oh I see

but you'll have to remember what order

what order I'm going round the room

is that all right?

yes I could do that.

So I've got my house when I was a child in my mind and I'm going to go round it now and put a crocodile on the doorstep

a crocodile on the table

a pincushion just inside on the mat

pincushion on the chair

pair of scissors in the sittingroom on the sofa

pair of scissors on the other chair

axe in the diningroom on the table

axe on the other chair

wristwatch

wristwatch

could you just in your head do you mind I can't

I'm not bothered by hearing yours

keep seeing your room in my

because I don't know where you lived as a child so it doesn't

so I can still say

yes if it helps and I'll just

thank you ok so wristwatch in the kitchen on the cooker
elephant on the stairs poundcoin in the bathroom biro on their
bed hedgehog on my bed tree in the attic

tree

makes ten. So now we go round

pick them up

on the doorstep crocodile

crocodile pincushion

pincushion yes scissors in the sittingroom

scissors wristwatch

no not yet

oh it's on the other

sh

so it's

axe

axe axe wristwatch

wristwatch

elephant

poundcoin

now where did I put?

oh

what?

bedroom

on top of the cd player

no in the bedroom I suddenly

biro

yes of course biro but I suddenly

what

saw my father

in his bedroom

my father getting dressed

he's not he wasn't

no it's nothing

nothing awful happened you're not remembering

no nothing like that at all I just suddenly saw him and

so when did you last

no it's just that he's dead and I don't

of course years ago I'd forgotten I'm

no it's nothing it's just he was there in the bedroom

and that's a memory is it

yes I suppose it is of course it's a memory from

from when you were little

yes because he's very I'm only half his size so

so is this like a new

yes a new memory and I'm seeing

you can see with your eyes when you were

say maybe four and the sunlight

sunlight

yes because it's sunny in the room shining in behind him and on
the floor on my feet

you can see your feet

I can see my feet when I was four

which isn't a memory you've always

no I've never

and you're sure it's not some horrible

some repressed no it's not it's just a memory isn't it

so the room faced east

yes it's morning in the room and I just saw it

some sort of crossed wire.

Because of course it's biro

biro

hedgehog

I've lost the hedgehog wait oh it's in the microwave I don't know where I went next oh I know on the pile of old newspapers it's a tree

tree in the attic.

So could we say the list straight off

I'm sure we could

and then do another list

lots of lists

and how do we keep the lists separate

I'm not sure yet I've got to

because I'll keep getting the hedgehog in the microwave

wait a minute I'll find out

find out what to do next.

DINNER

I did tell you

you didn't

I did I said Wednesday we're going to dinner with

but you didn't

yes because I remember because you said

all right I must have forgotten I'm sorry

yes you did

I'm sorry.

PIANO

Three people.

1.   This is Jennifer.

2.   Hello, Jennifer.

1.   Here's the piano. You can play the piano.

2.   I've never played the piano.

1.   You sit here.

He sits. He plays well and JENNIFER *sings. He gets up.*

2.   Hello.

1.   This is Jennifer.

2.   Hello, Jennifer.

FLASHBACK

Breathe

ah ah ah

just breathe

ah ah

I've got you, it's all right

ah

all right.

Thank you. Sorry. I keep seeing… I can see… I can't stop seeing…

I wish I could stop it for you.

Short of smashing in my skull.

They say time, you may be able to forget, even if it's a long time.

Once it's in there. Once you know that stuff.

5

LINGUIST

How many languages do you know?

To speak fluently

or a bit

well of course some languages I only know a few words, while others

take something like a table, take a table, how many languages can you

table table trapezi stol mesa meza tarang tabulka

That's so fantastic. Tabulka. Meza. They all mean table.

They all mean the same thing as each other.

Table.

Table means the same thing.

Yes, they all mean table.

Or they all mean meza.

Oh if you mean Chinese.

Or in fact Swahili.

I can't help feeling it actually is a table.

MATHS

I don't want to spend an evening with them again.

You like them. You like her.

He will keep making his point about mathematics not corresponding to reality because it's just a system our brains developed as we evolved in the world and we've had that argument.

Whereas maths is really true.

Yes.

Which is why if an equation wouldn't work without there being an infinite number of universes there really must be an infinite number of universes.

That sort of thing.

But we do only have our senses, don't we, to perceive with and maybe there's all sorts of other things we haven't evolved to perceive. Like an earthworm can't know about flying or a bird can't know about computers.

Don't let's have this conversation.

Why not go and see them and keep off the topic? We can argue about politics.

Because he won't keep off the topic, he likes trying to make me angry because he fancies you. And nobody understands what we're talking about and the evening's ruined and we all get drunk and I feel like shit in the morning and can't work.

Are you saying you never want to see them again?

He says maths is just consistent with itself. He keeps saying it doesn't mean anything.

What does it mean then?

All right, we'll go and see them.

She fancies you.

SEX

What sex evolved to do is get information from two sets of genes so you get offspring that's not identical to you. Otherwise you just keep getting the same thing over and over again like hydra or starfish. So sex essentially is information.

You don't think that while we're doing it do you?

It doesn't hurt to know it. Information and also love.

If you're lucky.

GOD

God gives your life meaning. You've said that.

Yes, so?

If there wasn't God there'd be no meaning to your existence?

And?

So does God have a higher god to give his existence meaning? and that god a higher god and that god

no of course not

of course not, so all this stuff he's done, he might find it all a bit meaningless. I'm surprised he's not depressed.

I don't think he minds whether he means anything or not. I don't think he thinks about it.

So why do you think about it?

I'm not God am I?

But I don't mind not meaning anything, does that make me God?

It makes you really annoying.

RASH

It's just a rash.

But why, why a rash?

There's all kinds of like detergents and animals and stuff in the air. Shall we have him tested?

He's trying to tell us something.

Oh come on.

Or he's trying not to tell us something.

Did you get the new cream?

CHILDREN

You can't have children?

No.

You can't have children?

No.

How did you find that out?

When I was married, it came up, we had tests and it was me.

So was that why?

No of course not.

I thought it was because she went off with the Spaniard.

She did

and she's got a baby now hasn't she, she and the Spaniard have got a bambino.

So it makes a difference does it?

SHRINK

It used to just be pain

the memories of what happened to you when you were a child and

and the things I wasn't letting myself remember of course

the things you'd

yes and now

so the analysis has stopped it hurting

not so much stopped

as what?

changed it into

changed it into?

transformed it

into what though?

It has meaning.

Because you see where it comes from?

partly that

and how it's affected the way you are?

partly that

and partly what?

It just has meaning now.

What does it mean?

It doesn't mean something. There isn't exactly another thing that it means.

Then what do you mean when you say it has meaning now?

You spoil it. You completely spoil everything. You always do.

That must be painful for you. You can take it to your analyst and have it turned into meaning.

6

THE CHILD WHO DIDN'T KNOW SORRY

You have to say you're sorry.

I'm not sorry.

But you know you hurt him. You have to say you're sorry.

I don't feel sorry.

You have to say it.

CLIMATE

I'm frightened.

Just walk instead of driving and don't take so many hot baths.

I'm frightened for the children.

There were those emails those scientists, I can't remember the detail

no it didn't make any difference in the end

no I think you're right, most scientists all agree it's a catastrophe. The question is how bad a catastrophe.

It's whether they drown or starve or get killed in the fights for water.

I'd choose drowning.

Are you really not going to take it seriously?

I don't know how to.

I don't know how to.

CENSOR

Page forty-two.

Page forty-two.

The sentence beginning 'On the 21st of May...'

Yes, I've got it.

I'm afraid that's going to have to go.

Why is that?

The Ministry of Defence considers it a breach of security.

It's not classified information.

That is nevertheless their view.

Have you got a lot of these?

About thirty.

Let's hear the next one then.

WIFE

But I am your wife.

You look like my wife.

That's because I am. Look, even that little birthmark behind my ear. Look.

Yes, I see it.

It's me. Darling sweet, it's me. I'm here.

No, she's gone. They've all gone.

Who's gone?

Everyone I know. Everyone who loved me.

No, I love you.

I don't want you to love me, I don't know you.

There's things only we know, aren't there. That day on the beach with the shells. You remember that?

Yes, of course.

And cabbages. Why is cabbages a funny word, we're the only ones who have cabbages as a joke because of what happened with the cabbages. Cabbages is a joke, yes?

Cabbages was a joke I shared with my wife. I miss my wife.

But I am… Let me touch you. If you'd see what it feels like to touch me. If we made love you'd know it was me because there are things we like to do and no one else would know that, if I was a stranger pretending to be her I wouldn't know those things, you'd feel you were back with me, you would I know, please.

You disgust me. You frighten me. What are you?

DECISION

I've written down all the reasons to leave the country and all the reasons to stay.

So how does that work out?

There's things on both sides.

How do you feel about it?

No, I'm trying to make a rational decision based on the facts.

Do you want me to decide for you?

Based on what? The facts don't add up.

I'd rather you stayed here. Does that help?

THE CHILD WHO DIDN'T KNOW PAIN

But what is it?

Pain is pain, it's just

if I pinch

aah, get off. But if I pinch you

nothing

nothing at all

but stop because I get bruises.

How come you don't

I never did when I was a baby

you were born like

yes and I used to chew my fingers

you mean chew?

and they got bandages put over or I'd chew them to the bone because you know how babies

put everything in their mouth

I'd put myself in my mouth because it wasn't any different.

And if you fell down

I threw myself down

because it didn't hurt

jumped down a whole flight of stairs because that was a quick way

and you were all right

broke both my legs and once when I went swimming there were rocks under the water and when I came out my legs were pouring blood because I hadn't felt

so you can't feel anything

emotions I feel feelings

but physical

not pain, no.

And why not?

because there's no signal going up to my brain

from your legs

from anywhere to my brain to say there's damage, it's hurting

so you never know what hurting is

so tell me what it's like.

Hurting is well it's pain, it's like uncomfortable but more, it's something you'd want to move away from but you can't, it's an intense sensation, it's hard to ignore it, it's very

but why would you mind that?

because it hurts. But no, sometimes pain's all right if it's not bad like if your gum's sore and you keep poking it with your tongue or you might cut your finger and you hardly notice, yes if you're doing something exciting, soldiers can lose a leg and not even know it

that's like me

yes but they know it afterwards. And bad pain

yes but why, what is it?

if someone's tortured if they give them electric shocks it's unbearable or if they've got cancer sometimes they want to die because my uncle

yes but I still don't know what it is about pain

it's just pain

but what is it?

You've been unhappy?

yes

if someone you love doesn't love you, you thought they loved you and they don't yes

or you've done something you wish you hadn't done it's too late now and you've hurt someone and there's nothing you can do to put it right

yes

does that help?

So it's like being unhappy but in your leg?

But it's also just what it is, like red is red and blue is blue.

But red isn't red, it's waves and it's red to us.

So there you are, that's what it's like.

Can I pinch you again?

EARTHQUAKE

Have you seen the earthquake? There's this building my god you think things are solid but they just break.

Yes I've seen it.

Imagine being in it, imagine you're lying on your back and there's this wall a few inches above your face and you can't sit up even an inch and if you do it might come down on you. And the air running out, you keep trying to get a deep breath but you can't breathe deeply enough because very soon there's going to be no more oxygen. And if you were injured if you're in pain while all that's going on and where are your family are they dead or in agony and will anyone come to get you out and how many hours or days, I'm just so upset by it.

I wouldn't want to be in it obviously, poor them of course. I mean I do know about it.

But you don't care.

I can't say I feel it, no. You really feel it?

I cried. Of course I feel it. I cried.

Ok.

And imagine the wave coming, imagine hearing it coming and running away and you can't get away, it came so fast did you see how fast it came?

Yes, I saw it.

You're not upset though.

That black wave with the cars in it was awesome.

7

CHINESE POETRY

'The girl waits at the door of her house on the mountain.'

What it literally says is 'mountain girl door'.

So maybe

A girl from the mountain is waiting outside my door. A girl climbs the mountain and comes to a door.

To get the girl you have to go through a door into the mountain.

The mountain is a door only a girl can open.

The girl's as big as a mountain and can't get through the door.

What's the next line?

MANIC

My god, look at that flower, thank you so much, have you ever seen such a red, red is blood and bullfights and seeing red is anger but red is joyful, red is celebration,

yes, I like it

in China red is lucky how lucky we are to have red flowers,

shall I get a vase?

in China white is death and here black is death but ghosts are white of course so a chessboard is death against death, and blood of course could be death but it's lifeblood isn't it, if you look at the flower it's so astounding

yes

it means so much to me that you gave me red flowers because red is so significant don't you think? it means stop and of course it means go because it's the colour of energy and red cars have the most accidents because people are excited by red or people who are already excited like to have red, I'd like to have red, I'll buy a red car this afternoon and we can go for a drive, we can go right up through the whole country don't you think, we can go to Scotland we can go to John o' Groats, did he eat a lot of porridge do you think? but we don't have to start from Land's End or Land's Beginning we should say if we start from there but we won't we'll start from here because here is always the place we start from, isn't that funny, and I need to drive along all the roads in the country because I have to see to the traffic because there are too many cars as everyone knows but our car won't be one too many you'll be quite safe, we'll make sure it's all flowing smoothly in every direction because cars do go in every direction possible and everything goes in every possible direction, so we'll find a vase for the flowers,

yes

I think a green vase because of the primary colours and if they were blue I'd put them in an orange vase and if they were yellow I'd put them in a purple vase, yellow and purple is Easter of course so that's why crocuses, and red and green is Christmas which isn't right now of course it's the wrong time of year, I might have to sort that out when I've got a minute.

GRIEF

Are you sleeping?

I wake up early but that's all right in the summer.

Eating?

Oh enough. Don't fuss.

I've never had someone die.

I'm sorry, I've nothing to say. Nothing seems very interesting.

He must have meant everything to you.

Maybe. We'll see.

FATE

I'm just saying you've got no choice

I have

you have of course you feel as if you have

I have got a choice

you've got a choice but you've no choice about what that choice is, you'll make whichever choice

whichever choice I want

whichever choice you want but you'll want what you want because you have to want what

I don't have to want

you do because of what you're like, that's what what you're like means that you're going to want what you want, because there's your genes and everything that's happened to you and everything else that's happening and all that stuff makes your brain be like that

like what?

like it is

what's it like?

I don't know of course I don't know nobody knows, but if someone could have that information they'd know exactly what you were going to

they can't know

you're crying about it now

I'm not

I knew you would.

But there's random

oh there's random

there's random particles you can't

if you think you're like a random particle

no but

if you think you're a random particle just fizzing

but you can't predict even where

if you think free will is a random particle there's nothing very noble

I didn't say noble

so what is free will if it's not what you're like?

No one could possibly have all that information.

No, of course not.

So maybe that's all right.

I think it's fine. But it does change how you feel, don't you think?

I feel a bit funny

yes you feel as if you're hurtling

hurtling through my life

like the front seat of a roller-coast

but I feel like I'm choosing

yes of course

but I feel like I'm in the front seat of a roller-coaster.

STONE

He's got a special stone.

Is that what he's holding?

Yes he's always got it in his hand.

I know he's always holding

never puts it down

have you seen it?

saw it once

how

made him open his

shall we get it?

I think he needs it

yes shall we get it?

They get the stone and throw it away.

Go and get it then

it's over there

will he know which one?

he can get another one

he might want that one

shall we get him one?

Here have a stone

have another stone

have a stone

Throwing them.

VIRTUAL

I don't care what you say

no but listen

I've never felt like this

that's not the point what you feel

it's the only

because she doesn't exist

I'm not listening.

She doesn't

have you seen her?

yes I've seen her but she doesn't

have you talked to her?

I don't want to talk to

then what do you know about it?

she's not a real

so?

so you admit she's not

she exists she still exists

fine all right she exists but so does your shoe or a can of

you're saying she's no different than a shoe?

she's got no more feelings than

what do you know about

she's a thing she's a thing.

Look I appreciate your concern but just

look

she's beautiful she's intelligent she understands me

she doesn't understand you

she listens to me she likes my poems she's the only

doesn't understand any

she reads my mind she's sensitive to my every

but she's virtual

so?

so she's not

I can't believe just because someone's not flesh and blood you'd she's just information

and what are you if you're not

yes I know we're

so we're information our genes our

yes but she hasn't

what?

hasn't got an inside to her mind she's not conscious she can't

how do you know she

she's a computer she's a computer game she's not

and can you tell that from what she says?

I don't need to

but can you tell

because she can't

she might and how could she prove it because you wouldn't
believe

I certainly wouldn't

because she says she has

what, thoughts

of course thoughts feelings because she's that complicated she
says she loves

she can't possibly

we know people won't understand but we don't care what you

and what about sex

what about

she hasn't got a body

she's got a fantastic

but not a body you can

she's not in this country at the moment

she can't ever

and the sex is great

it's virtual

it's virtual and great

but she never feels

I don't care what you say

no but listen

I've never felt like this about anyone.

SMALL THING

What are you looking at?

A snail.

Is that the same snail?

Yes. I've been looking at it for a while.

And?

I'm just looking at it.

LAST SCENE

FACTS

Who was president of Coca-Cola from nineteen twenty-five to seven?

HB Jones.

What is the smallest village in Central Asia?

Qat.

Where would you see a huish?

In a gnu's fur.

How many diamonds were mined in 1957?

Sixty thousand four hundred and twenty-eight.

Name two traditional ingredients of poulash.

Duck and fennel.

In 1647 what day was the battle of Stoneham?

June the third. Tuesday.

How far is it from here to the quasar d 66?

Three point four billion light years.

What sound does a capercaillie make?

Aaaah.

Who had the longest hair?

Matilda Lucas.

Of?

Brighouse, Connecticut.

What colour is the caterpillar of the brown-haired bat moth?

Pale orange with black stripes.

Do you love me?

Don't do that.

What is the formula that disproves Gödel's theorem?

X bracket a over t minus pi sigma close bracket to the power of ten minus n to the power of minus one squared

What is a plok?

A stringed instrument played by the Larts of the the Gobi Desert

By what name do we usually refer to Oceanus Australensis Picardia?

I do yes I do. Sea anemone.

RANDOM

RANDOM

These things can happen in any section. DEPRESSION *is an essential part of the play. The other random items are optional.*

DEPRESSION

Each of these is a separate random item. Not all of them need to be used. Each is said by one person to another who doesn't respond. The characters can be the same each time, or the depressed person can be the same and the others different, or they can all be different.

we could go for a walk it's a beautiful

there's an exhibition of expressionist

chicken tikka masala

programme starts at 6.40 or if you'd rather we could

glass of red or

thinking of taking one of the kittens there's a ginger one or a

maybe you could read them a story tonight or

the difficulty of getting the Israelis and Palestinians to

and he only has two months to live so I thought we could

a fountain of antimatter in the Milky Way that nobody knew

OPTIONAL

SEMAPHORE

MORSE

SIGN LANGUAGE

BIRDSONG

DANCE

FLAGS

PAINTING

Someone has a large canvas and is flicking paint at it.

PIG LATIN

Ancay ouyay eakspay igpay atinlay?

SANTA

Father Christmas lands his sleigh on the roof and comes down
the chimney with his big sack of toys and he'll put presents in
your stocking

TABLES

Seven sevens are forty-nine, seven eights are fifty-six, seven nines are sixty-three, seven tens are seventy, seven elevens are seventy-seven, seven twelves are eighty-four, seven thirteens are ninety-one

GENES

AGT TCG AGC CCT TGA CTT GAT TGT GCA TAC
CGT GCT TGA GTC ATG TTG CAC AAC TTG TCG
GTC TCA GTA TGC CCG TGA AAT GTA CAT GTC
CGG TCC GAA TCT GAT TGC CCT TTG TGG AAC
TGT GTG GCA TAG CTA GCC TGG GAC CCT TTG
GGC TGC ACT TGA TTG TCA CCA GGT TGT TCT
GTT GAA TCA TGA TCG GAC CCA CGT CGG CTG
GCC GAC TTT GAC CGG AGT GGT TGT ACC TTG
GTC AGG AAT TGA ACG

DOG

Come. Sit. Stay. Come. Good dog. Fetch. Drop it. Fetch. Good dog. Roll over. Good dog. Come. Heel. No. Come.

KEYS

You don't know where I put the car keys, do you?

MAGAZINE

she's lost two stone… he was going to leave her… look, he's coming out of a club with an unnamed blonde…

GOOGLE

There's a train at 4.22 gets in at half-past eight.

TWITTER

He's in the kitchen cooking spaghetti and he's upset about the news from Tripoli.

ZEN

What's the sound of one hand clapping? I've heard that one.

COLD

Someone sneezes.

SILENCE

This can happen more than once, for different lengths of time.

DING DONG THE WICKED

Ding Dong the Wicked was first performed at the Royal Court Theatre Downstairs, London, on 1 October 2012. The cast was as follows:

A QUIET MAN/A MAN WHO BITES HIS NAILS
John Marquez

A WOMAN IN BLUE/A DRUNK WOMAN
Sophie Stanton

YOUNG WOMAN HOLDING A FLOWER/
YOUNG WOMAN WITH A CIGARETTE
Claire Foy

AN OVERWEIGHT MAN/A MAN WHO IS A WRECK
Stuart McQuarrie

A WOMAN WHO BITES/A WOMAN WITH A LIMP
Jennie Stoller

A PALE YOUNG MAN/A SPEEDY YOUNG MAN
Daniel Kendrick

Director	Dominic Cooke
Lighting Designer	Jack Williams
Sound Designer	Alexander Caplen

Characters
in order of appearance

1.

A QUIET MAN, *forty-five*
A WOMAN IN BLUE, *late forties*
A YOUNG WOMAN CARRYING A FLOWER, *twenties,
    girlfriend of the pale young man*
AN OVERWEIGHT MAN, *fifty-plus, husband of the woman in blue,
    brother of the quiet man*
A WOMAN WHO BITES, *seventies, mother of the overweight man
    and the quiet man*
A PALE YOUNG MAN, *twenties, a soldier, son of the overweight man
    and the woman in blue*

2.

A YOUNG WOMAN WITH A CIGARETTE, *twenties*
A MAN WHO BITES HIS NAILS, *forty-five, her husband*
A DRUNK WOMAN, *late forties, her mother*
A WOMAN WITH A LIMP, *seventies, her grandmother*
A SPEEDY YOUNG MAN, *twenties, a soldier, brother of the man
    who bites his nails*
A MAN WHO IS A WRECK, *fifty-plus, a neighbour*

The actors double the parts.

Place

1. A living room.

2. A living room in another country.

1.

A living room. There is a door leading to the rest of the house, a front door and a window. There is a tv but we can't see the screen or hear the sound.

A QUIET MAN, *about forty-five, is alone in the room. There is a plastic sheet on the floor and a large strong bin bag.*

Doorbell. The QUIET MAN *opens the front door, taking out a gun.*

QUIET MAN	Come in.
	The QUIET MAN *shoots someone, who falls dead. The* QUIET MAN *puts the body and the bloodstained plastic sheet in the bag, and leaves with the bag by the front door.*
	Time passes.
	Doorbell. A WOMAN IN BLUE, *late forties, comes from inside and opens the street door. A* YOUNG WOMAN CARRYING A FLOWER *comes in, they embrace.*
YW *w* FLOWER	All right?
W *in* BLUE	I am, he is, guess who's making a fuss. Just don't get him started.
FLOWER	It's because he's suffered, isn't it, I know he has.
BLUE	I get tired of it.
FLOWER	Of course.
BLUE	I'm not saying he's wrong.
FLOWER	You're sensible, that's what it is.
BLUE	Mind you.
FLOWER	Oh I'm not saying…

BLUE	There's someone kept calling me names when I was at school, jellybelly, doubletrouble – just a bit overweight – and one day I pushed her so she fell down in a puddle and before she could get herself sorted out I jumped right on her and I got a handful of mud and stuffed it in her mouth.
FLOWER	She was asking for it.
BLUE	She was pretty but she was skinny. She's the one with the problem.
FLOWER	Did I hear someone crying?
BLUE	She's just calming down. You can't let them think they've got you where they want you. You have to break their spirit. It doesn't take long.

An OVERWEIGHT MAN, *about fifty, husband of the woman in blue, enters from indoors and goes to the window.*

OVERWEIGHT	What's happened?
BLUE	We keep watch all the time so they don't get away with anything.
FLOWER	Is it bad?
BLUE	Music day and night.
FLOWER	They're such beautiful trees too.
OVERWEIGHT	Bastards. Bastards. They want to destroy us.
BLUE	(*To* FLOWER.) I did tell you.
OVERWEIGHT	I'll kill them. Help me.
BLUE	Everything's all right. It's all right. We have a visitor.

OVERWEIGHT	Come to see him off, have you? He's going to be a hero. It's a big cause. Is he a big enough man?
BLUE	(*To* FLOWER.) He's in his room. He'd like to see you.
	The YOUNG WOMAN CARRYING A FLOWER *exits indoors.*
	She's not crying any more. Shall I get her?
OVERWEIGHT	I've something to say to you.
BLUE	You've nothing to say, I know what you get up to.
OVERWEIGHT	It's not surprising, I'm not the one who started this.
BLUE	I'm not the one breaking up our marriage, don't try and put it on me.
OVERWEIGHT	You want to break it up, do you?
BLUE	I didn't say that.
OVERWEIGHT	You want it, you can have it, it's your idea remember that.
BLUE	No one could blame me. I've been hurt. You're a monster. Just let it go. I'm past caring now.
OVERWEIGHT	What's happening out there?
BLUE	Another thing, I've had enough of your brother. He's a criminal. I don't need this. And drinking again.
OVERWEIGHT	He's not staying forever.
BLUE	How long's forever? How long's he not staying for?
OVERWEIGHT	Will you stop shouting at me?
BLUE	I didn't raise my voice. Did I raise my voice?

OVERWEIGHT	I'm not listening.
BLUE	I know you're not.
OVERWEIGHT	It's his last day. It could be a peaceful time.
BLUE	And whose fault is it? I'm basically a very peaceful person.
OVERWEIGHT	You?
BLUE	Aren't I?
OVERWEIGHT	Yes, you are.
BLUE	I'm what?
OVERWEIGHT	A peaceful person. Am I? What do you think?
BLUE	Yes.
OVERWEIGHT	Good. You have to forgive me because I mean well.
BLUE	There then. There, my dear. Shall we let her out?
OVERWEIGHT	No, let's have some peace.

The QUIET MAN *lets himself in through the front door. He is the brother of the overweight man.*

QUIET MAN	Gone?
BLUE	He'll be down in a minute.
QUIET MAN	Drink?
BLUE	You drink too much.
QUIET MAN	Drink?
BLUE	Might as well.
QUIET MAN	Bastard came up on the inside so I cut in front to show him and he nearly drove me off the road.

BLUE   (*To* OVERWEIGHT.) Go and get him. I
                want to see him.

OVERWEIGHT   I was about fifteen, there was a dead
                dog, the body was by the road, and I
                thought, asleep, no, that's dead, it was
                getting squashy, there was a lot of flies,
                and I thought that's really dead, and I
                suddenly thought I could do that, if it
                really helped my country and what I
                believe in and the people I love and our
                way of life which is threatened, if I
                could take some of those bastards with
                me I could be really happy to be dead,
                except I didn't expect to be happy, I
                expect to be nothing, but happy to do
                something that could make me end up
                dead, I could do that.

                The OVERWEIGHT MAN *goes by the*
                inside door.

QUIET MAN   You know what he did.

BLUE   I don't want to talk about that.

QUIET MAN   Nobody talks about that.

BLUE   He always tells that story.

QUIET MAN   Yes, that's the bit he tells.

                Pause.

BLUE   We mustn't.

QUIET MAN   I know but we have to.

BLUE   He's just as bad.

QUIET MAN   He's insane.

BLUE   Oh god, I want you so much.

QUIET MAN   I want you so much.

BLUE   I want you so much too.

A WOMAN WHO BITES, *seventies,*
mother of the overweight man and the quiet
man, enters from indoors.

W WHO BITES	Where is he?
BLUE	He'll be down in a minute.
QUIET MAN	Drink?
BITES	Are we celebrating? Celebrating sending another one off to be killed?
BLUE	Celebrating maybe he'll kill some of them.
BITES	My darling was completely destroyed. There was nothing left.
BLUE	Yes, don't get excited.
BITES	They've got graves to go to, you stupid child. Killing's not enough.

The OVERWEIGHT MAN *comes back in.*

OVERWEIGHT	There's nothing I inherited except my father's hair and his lefthandedness. Everything I got I earned. And the government want to take that away. The hero's coming.
BLUE	I'm going to let her out.
OVERWEIGHT	I said no.
QUIET MAN	Is she shut in her room again?
BLUE	Her parents know what to do, thank you.

A PALE YOUNG MAN, *son of the*
overweight man and the woman in blue, and the
YOUNG WOMAN CARRYING A
FLOWER *enter from indoors. He is wearing*
military uniform and holding the flower.

BITES	Here we are.
OVERWEIGHT	Have you ever seen a man dead?
QUIET MAN	(*Offering*) Drink?
PALE YM	It's fine because I believe in what we're doing.
BITES	You're a good boy.
OVERWEIGHT	His grandfather was a missionary. He gave his life bringing the truth.
FLOWER	I do think it's right to try to be good.
BLUE	You're drinking too much.
QUIET MAN	And?
OVERWEIGHT	That's the most important thing, a clear conscience.
BITES	They're pus you have to kill with disinfectant. Vermin.
QUIET MAN	Drink?
BLUE	(*To* FLOWER.) They want to build ugly little houses right in the middle of the view. It's lovely there. It's ancient. I won't take it. I'm not the type.
BITES	(*To* FLOWER.) Did you know my son was killed? Do you know about it?
FLOWER	Yes, I'm sorry.
OVERWEIGHT	So you're here to say goodbye.
FLOWER	Yes, I keep crying.
PALE	She'll forget all about me.
FLOWER	He doesn't mean that.
PALE	It's my beautiful country, that's what it is.
BLUE	Listen. Listen.

OVERWEIGHT	Listen. Look. Blood

They all turn to the tv. We can't see the screen or hear what's said. They listen and look, then explode in triumph.

Dead.

BLUE	Yes!
FLOWER	What?
QUIET MAN	They've got him.
BITES	He's dead.
BLUE	Did you hear that?
OVERWEIGHT	Like a dog.
PALE	Yaaay.

They all start a chant, which goes on for some time, continuing while other things are said.

ALL	Zig zig zig, zag zag zag, zig zig zig, zag zag zag…
BITES	Oh god oh god oh god
BLUE	(*To* PALE.) Specially for you.
OVERWEIGHT	Go go go.

The chant dies down, laughter.

FLOWER	I can't help feeling
QUIET MAN	This calls for a drink. Shall we let her out?
OVERWEIGHT	Listen!

The OVERWEIGHT MAN *goes to the window.*

Look! The trees!

The OVERWEIGHT MAN *rushes off indoors* (*to the garden*) *followed by the* WOMAN IN BLUE *and the* QUIET MAN.

PALE   Can't help feeling what?

FLOWER   Nothing.

PALE   What?

FLOWER   A bit sorry for him.

PALE   I can. Do you love me?

FLOWER   Yes. Do you love me?

PALE   Yes. That's good then.

BITES   Where's everyone gone?

FLOWER   I think people should try to forgive each other.

PALE   We can't do that.

FLOWER   No, I know.

PALE   I'll tell you something. If you love me.

FLOWER   What?

BITES   What are you whispering about?

FLOWER   Tell me.

PALE   I don't want to do it. I don't think I can do it.

FLOWER   You can.

PALE   I don't want to.

The QUIET MAN *comes back.*

QUIET MAN   False alarm. Want a drink?

PALE   Not now.

FLOWER   Yes, please.

QUIET   (*To* PALE.) You'll get drunk a lot if you
                    get the chance.

BITES   There's my brave boy. Bite.

FLOWER   I'm sorry, I can't stop crying.

PALE   Zig zig zig.

2.

Another country. A living room. It is identical and the furniture is identical except it's in different positions.

A MAN WHO BITES HIS NAILS, *about forty-five, and a*
YOUNG WOMAN WITH A CIGARETTE.

YW *w* CIG	It's a big cause.
MAN NAILS	Have you ever seen a man dead?
CIG	Will you stop shouting at me?
NAILS	Did I raise my voice?
CIG	I'm not the one breaking up our marriage.
NAILS	You want it to break up, do you?
CIG	I get tired of it.
NAILS	I do think it's right to try to be good.
CIG	Do you love me?
NAILS	Yes.
CIG	It's my beautiful country, that's what it is.
NAILS	Do you love me?
CIG	What do you think?
NAILS	I want you so much.
CIG	I want you so much too.
NAILS	He'll be down in a minute.
CIG	I've had enough of your brother.
NAILS	He's insane.
CIG	He's going to be a hero.

NAILS	You know what he did?
	Doorbell. The YOUNG WOMAN WITH A CIGARETTE *opens the street door and a* DRUNK WOMAN, *late forties, her mother, and a* WOMAN WITH A LIMP, *seventies, her grandmother, come in, embracing her.*
DRUNK W	Here we are.
CIG	Come to see him off? He's in his room.
NAILS	Drink?
DRUNK	Are we celebrating? I am.
WOMAN *w* LIMP	Did I hear crying? Is she shut in her room again?
CIG	She's the one with a problem.
DRUNK	Bastard came up on the inside so I cut in front to show him and he nearly drove me off the road. There was a dead dog.
NAILS	You?
DRUNK	No one could blame me.
CIG	Drinking again.
DRUNK	I don't want to talk about that.
CIG	No, I know.
DRUNK	Guess who's making a fuss. You drink too much.
LIMP	She's not crying any more.
CIG	Her parents know what to do, thank you.
	A SPEEDY YOUNG MAN, *brother of the man who bites his nails, enters from indoors. He is wearing a military uniform, not the same as the pale young man wore in 1.*

DRUNK	The hero's coming.
SPEEDY YM	So you're here to say goodbye.
DRUNK	Celebrating. You're a good boy. Maybe he'll kill some of them.
NAILS	Don't get excited.
SPEEDY	I'll kill them all right.
CIG	Killing's not enough.
SPEEDY	Drink?
DRUNK	Let's. It's his last day.
CIG	We keep watch all the time so they can't get away with anything. You can't let them think they've got you where they want you. They're vermin.
NAILS	I can't help feeling…
CIG	What?
NAILS	Nothing. Just let it go.
CIG	I'm not the one that started this. Don't try and put it on me.
NAILS	I didn't say that.
CIG	I believe in what we're doing.
LIMP	Shall we let her out? Shall I get her?
CIG	There's someone kept calling me names when I was at school, I was about fifteen, and one day I jumped right on her.
SPEEDY	Bastards.
CIG	You have to break their spirit.
SPEEDY	The body was by the road right in the middle of the view and I thought, that's dead, that's really dead, it was getting squashy, there was a lot of flies, and

	I suddenly thought I could do that if it really helped my country, if I could take some of those bastards out.
CIG	I could do that.
NAILS	You want it.
SPEEDY	I'm basically a very peaceful person. But we have to.
CIG	I know.
DRUNK	There's my brave boy. He is.
SPEEDY	There was nothing left. She was asking for it. She fell down. And before she could get herself sorted out, I stuffed it in her mouth. I don't expect to be happy. But happy to do something.
NAILS	And that's the bit he tells. I know what you get up to. You're a monster.
CIG	He doesn't mean that.
SPEEDY	I'm what?
CIG	He's just as bad.
NAILS	Am I?
CIG	Yes, you are. Nobody talks about that.
SPEEDY	A clear conscience?
CIG	A peaceful person. (*To* NAILS.) You've nothing to say.
NAILS	If I did…
SPEEDY	Is it bad?
NAILS	Of course.
SPEEDY	It's not surprising. Tell me.
NAILS	I don't think I can.

CIG   Mind you, I'm not saying he's wrong. It's
               fine because…

NAILS   Because I mean well?

DRUNK   What are you whispering about? Do you
               know they want to build ugly little
               houses? They're such beautiful trees too.
               And the government wants to take that
               away. Bastards. Everything I earned.

CIG   You're drinking too much. I'm not
               listening.

DRUNK   What do you know about it, you stupid
               child? There's nothing I inherited except
               my father's lefthandedness.

LIMP   And his hair.

DRUNK   Can't help feeling what… Our way of
               life. It's the trees. And what I believe in,
               which is threatened.

LIMP   Yes, that's the most important thing.

DRUNK   I keep crying.

LIMP   (Of DRUNK.) Everything's all right.
               She's just calming down.

DRUNK   Bastards. I'll tell you something. You
               have to kill.

CIG   Drink, drink, specially for you. You can
               have it. Get drunk. I'm past caring.

NAILS   Listen.

CIG   What's happened?

SPEEDY   Listen. Look. They've got him.

               *They all turn to the tv. We can't see the screen
               or hear what's said. They listen and look then
               explode in triumph.*

DRUNK   Oh.

LIMP	Gone.
SPEEDY	Dead.
CIG	That's dead, that's really dead.
NAILS	Did you hear that?
DRUNK	Dog.
	They all start a chant which goes on for some time, continuing while other things are said.
ALL	Zig zig zig, zag zag zag, zig zig zig, zag zag zag...
DRUNK	Drink.
SPEEDY	(*To* CIG *secretly.*) I want you so much
CIG	(*To* SPEEDY *secretly.*) I said no.
LIMP	He's dead. Oh god.
SPEEDY	(*To* CIG *secretly.*) You're sensible, that's what it is.
DRUNK	Go go go.
	The chant dies down, laughter.
NAILS	This calls for a drink.
DRUNK	Celebrating.
NAILS	It could be a peaceful time now.
CIG	No, it's ancient.
NAILS	I think people should try to forgive each other.
SPEEDY	Is he a big enough man to forgive me?
LIMP	(*Aside to* DRUNK.) Shall we let her out? I'm going to let her out.
DRUNK	(*Aside to* LIMP.) You're not. We mustn't. We can't do that.
LIMP	(*Aside to* DRUNK.) I can.

NAILS	(*To* SPEEDY.) Might as well.
CIG	That's good then. And?
SPEEDY	I'm not the type.

Banging about outside then banging at the front door and ringing of doorbell. The WOMAN WITH A LIMP *gets up unnoticed except by the* DRUNK WOMAN *and exits indoors.*

What's happening out there?

The SPEEDY YOUNG MAN *produces a gun.*

NAILS	No. It's your idea.

More banging at the door.

DRUNK	Oh god.

The MAN WHO BITES HIS NAILS *opens the front door. A* MAN WHO IS A WRECK *comes in. He is very bedraggled and carries a large strong bin bag full of possessions. The* SPEEDY YOUNG MAN *puts the gun away.*

CIG	False alarm. We have a visitor.
NAILS	It's all right. I did tell you.
WRECK	(*Of himself.*) He'd like to see you.
SPEEDY	Just don't get him started.
CIG	He's not staying. Not now.
WRECK	Aren't I? I've something to say to you.
DRUNK	It's because he's suffered isn't it.
CIG	I know he has. He's a criminal.
DRUNK	A bit sorry for him. His grandfather was a missionary.
WRECK	Listen. My darling was completely destroyed. It doesn't take long. A puddle.

Blood. A handful of mud. There, my
dear. She was skinny but she was pretty.
Gone.

CIG   He always tells that story.

NAILS   How long's he not staying for?

WRECK   Did you know my son was killed? I won't
               take it. He gave his life bringing the
               truth. They've got graves to go to. You
               have. And whose fault is it? I'm not
               saying.

DRUNK   Want a drink?

WRECK   I can't stop crying. Oh god. Yes please.
               I'm sorry, I'm sorry. Sending another
               one off to be killed? If you love me. If
               you get the chance. With me. Zig zig zig.

               The WOMAN WITH A LIMP *comes
               back.*

LIMP   (*To* DRUNK.) Asleep.

WRECK   Just a bit overweight. Jellybelly,
               doubletrouble. Another thing, I've been
               hurt. A lot. Bastards. (*Pulling up his shirt.*) I
               got I got… Help me. Like a bite. Pus.
               With disinfectant. Could make me end
               up dead.

DRUNK   There then.

CIG   I don't need this.

LIMP   I could be really happy to be dead. Have
               some peace. She'll forget all about me.
               It's lovely there. Music day and night.
               Forever.

SPEEDY   I expect to be nothing. I pushed her in
               and… and someone… I didn't raise my
               voice. They want to destroy us,
               remember that.

LIMP	How long's forever?
DRUNK	What?
WRECK	I want to see him. Where's everyone gone? The people I love. Where is he? Go and get him.

Doorbell. The SPEEDY YOUNG MAN *has the gun again. The* YOUNG WOMAN WITH A CIGARETTE *takes it from him.*

SPEEDY	Yes. Do it.
CIG	I don't want to do it.
SPEEDY	You can.
CIG	Yes. Good. I don't want to. Yes.
NAILS	And?
DRUNK	Zig zig zig.
NAILS	Come in.

The MAN WHO BITES HIS NAILS *starts to open the front door.*

Black.

End.

HERE WE GO

Here We Go was first performed in the Lyttelton auditorium of the National Theatre, London, on 27 November 2015 (previews from 25 November). The cast was as follows:

Madeline Appiah
Susan Engel
Patrick Godfrey
Hazel Holder
Joshua James
Amanda Lawrence
Stuart McQuarrie
Eleanor Matsuura
Alan Williams

Director	Dominic Cooke
Designer	Vicki Mortimer
Lighting Designer	Guy Hoare
Sound Designer	Christopher Shutt

Note

The number of actors can vary in different productions. Not fewer than three in the first scene and not more than eight – five or six is probably good. Age and gender can also be decided. The character in After can be but needn't be the man whose funeral it is in the first scene. Same with Getting There, and the carer may or may not be someone we've met before.

1. HERE WE GO

The speeches at the end of the scene are to be inserted at random during the dialogue. There are ten – use as many as you need for each character to have one.

The place is a party after a funeral.

We miss him

of course

everyone

but his closest

because friendship was

wider range of acquaintance than anyone I've ever

gift

closeness

listened

and so witty I remember him saying

listened and understood

always seemed

though of course *are* you any wiser when you're older I feel sixteen all the time

all he'd lived through

the war the war not so many people left who

and Spain even imagine

what how old

no he did

and he never actually joined the party because of what they did
to the anarchists so

not that he was an anarchist

unless sexually

well yes there

and is the third wife here are they all

in the red hat

isn't that the daughter?

no the big red

and is that her partner with the beard?

all the women seem

yes they all kiss but I wonder

except of course

she's keeping very quiet

love of his life

they say

though he was an old goat

of course

such charm was the thing

yes because he didn't look

oh when he was young

none of us can remember

well I can

of course

he was a vision at thirty

and photos photos have you seen there are some on the table in
the

yes on a horse, about twelve

but his mind

yes his mind

extraordinary mind

literature of course but also

literature of France, Spain, Russia, every South American

physics, he had an extremely scientific

could have been

never fully

an mp in the fifties

I never knew

oh yes

which party

well obviously

yes but he was a libertarian

man of the left

always fell out

a bit too much of an individualist some might

just quarrelsome

but then he'd make it up with a bunch of flowers

I always remember a time he

and did you meet his friend Bill?

who isn't here or is he?

would we recognise?

heavy drinker

he put it away himself

but could always carry

champagne in hospital

so wonderful

never complained

well he did

terrible temper

I never saw

swore at the nurses

well I suppose anyone

yes pain

pain does change

horrible to see

morphine

can make you feel very happy, when I broke my pelvis

or sick

confused

sounded as if he was demented but of course we knew
it was

though he always did have a temper

I never saw

perhaps you didn't annoy

only the people who were closest

no, people he didn't know, cold-callers

van drivers

dogs

dogs?

he hated

never knew that

cats cats cats

yes what's going to happen

his daughter said she could take the old ginger tom but

in a flat?

cats like places of course more than people, they

your cat?

stopped being sick everywhere thank god, the vet's bills

and how are you keeping now you're

yes fantastic

wonderful job

New York in the morning so I can't stay too long I've got to

promotion

still hoping

painting

out of work so long now I

keeping busy

your new partner I hear

getting married

and you always said

yes but love when it really

yes

you don't quite expect

so happy for you

yes after all those

and we're expecting a baby in September but don't

so great

just close friends till

of course

another drink

have to remember I'm driving so

see all these people

yes because we hardly ever

and so many people I've never set eyes

all his different walks of

who've known him for sixty years

only met him last summer but he

talking to one of the carers

closer to him at the end I think than

well someone who washes

and wipes

you do love who you look after and who looks after you like
that's how with babies

or cats

all one way with cats

no stroking them reduces our

lovely service

favourite

but he wasn't a Christian surely or was it his

but what do you do?

plenty of people nowadays, pop songs, poems

yes despite everything he was rather

I don't think he cared, he's not the type who'd plan

no, plan their own service, oh dear

must keep an eye on the time

far to go?

came on the M23 and the roadworks at junction

go back through

long way round

stay overnight

long day tomorrow

I did cry

no I never actually have at a funeral

what sort of

self-pity and anger mainly I'm afraid, so

but that sort of lofty

uplifting

some bits of music

but not today's for me

no but the thought

yes hard to believe he's gone even though

it comes at you suddenly doesn't it

like stepping on a rake

I know after my mother

well parents of course are a different

not really

because then you're next

but you think your friend's still there in a different city and not
seeing them is

yes and then it hits you you'll never

and I find I can't remember voices

no not for long

we should all be recorded

please no, photographs are bad enough

oh but I love

let it go and just remember whatever we

the oddest things

can see him standing on one leg, I think it was in France were you there

no I never went to that house just to the one in what was that street?

very funny

he was

he could tell a joke

yes I can never remember

One of these is spoken by each of the characters directly to the audience.
They should be inserted randomly into the previous dialogue in any order.
The number of years later can be adjusted if necessary to make sense for the
characters.

I die the next day. I'm knocked over by a motorbike crossing a road in North London. I think I can get over while the light's red but I'm looking for cars. I'm dead before the ambulance comes and it comes very quickly.

I die eleven years later. I have a heart attack swimming in the North Sea in January. I'd done it before all right.

I die thirty-eight years later of lung cancer. I hadn't realised before that you have different kinds of cancer depending on where it starts so you can have breast cancer in your brain, and I have lung cancer in my liver. I don't find the pain relief as helpful as I'd hoped.

I die five years later stabbed by an intruder. I keep a knife by the bed and when I brandish it he snatches it. He's shocked by the blood, he's saying sorry sorry and then I pass out.

I die twenty-six years later. I slip over on the icy steps going to put out the rubbish and break my hip, and my chest gets worse lying in bed. I have given up smoking but a bit late.

I die forty years later in my sleep, which is a relief. I was expecting to live to see the baby.

I die seven years later of a brain tumour. It takes a while for the doctors to pay attention to the headaches but maybe it would have spread anyway.

I die sixty-two years later. More and more things aren't working. They put pneumonia on the death certificate.

I die twenty-three years later after nine years of Alzheimer's. I don't know anyone who's there.

I die six months later. I hang myself. I should have thought about who'd find me.

2. AFTER

One person. Very fast.

Falling falling down the tunnel down the tunnel a tunnel a light a train a tube train aaah coming to kill me

but I'm already dead is that right and ah here I am arrived somewhere and hello is that grandpa?

surely not greater light and further shore no

but is this the pearly gates yes look actual pearls and that's St Peter beard key

but I don't believe anything like

and it's gone is anyone there hello

there must be vast numbers of us that's a comfort far more than the living

except of course there used to be fewer living at any one time so maybe the living now equal all the dead could that be but even so there are billions right back to cave and where are they

oh there they are here we are I'm just a speck of sand in a desert oh

or what is this are we all standing on the Isle of Wight it's worse than the tube at rush hour I can't get my face away from his back I don't want

ah that's better they've gone I'm on my own

I'm on my own

and what's happened to me what's going to happen I always was
afraid despite everything there'd be a judgement and I'd be a
goat not a sheep thinking of those herds in North Africa where
they're mixed together and it can be hard to tell I understood
the metaphor then very good

and I think they don't emphasise hell these days but you can't be
sure because there's nothing kind about the universe just
rushing apart

and even our little place in it we evolved to belong has
hurricanes and cancer and is kind for some but often unkind
and they have to live with foul water or wake up in dread and
what would it be like to have to live your life as someone
obsessed with having sex with children or wanting to kill what
would you do with that

and it might not be fair to punish them but it may not be fair
because the universe isn't so who says god is if there is one here
somewhere

and hell used to be mediaeval tortures pincers and fire
and we thought god can't do that because no one would do that

but we know people do just that sort of thing quite a lot so
maybe there is a hell of arms chopped off and piles of bodies
with bags on their heads and hanging upside down ah why
shouldn't I be one of the people who deserve that

if deserving comes into it it might be random

because I'm the rich camel who can't get through compared to
oh I know there's mega how reassuring yachts but no I was
comfortable comfortable in my life chicken and a warm bed

and how much good did I very little because I was always loving
someone or organising something or looking at trees or having a
quiet sit-down with the paper and I'm sorry I'm sorry

or is it purgatory do they have that still where it's burned out of
you not for ever yes I can feel it getting hotter the blast of it on
my

ridiculous I don't believe it of course never did that's not
happening there's plenty of other something completely

yes here comes aah his head's what a wild dog fox jackal that's it
not a mask he's

and that one's a bird ibis long curved sharp I'm sorry I'm sorry

and here are the scales there's a feather in one pan so I take out
my heart and put it in the other and surely it can't be light as a
feather and if it weighs the pan down I get thrown to that lion
hippo crocodile and will I pass out as I feel its hot breath
sometimes people go into a swoon of shock when an animal has
them in its mouth National Geographic probably and then I
would really be dead and gone I suppose

which ancient religion is this anyway Egypt

surely I must be in for something more Nordic

Thor with a thunderbolt

valhalla or is that just for war heroes yes there they are sitting
round the table drunk and roaring not my idea of fun

and for illness or old age here's a blue black giantess come to
take me somewhere bleaker maybe a cold beach with a wind I
once went swimming I'd rather a warm Greek white stones can
I have that and is that Charon in the boat I can get in wobble sit
down and over the dark river we go

I've always been scared of guard dogs so I hope Cerberus

and do I have to gibber with those bloodless dead did Odysseus
go to see them yes I can see him coming now and here we are
all stretching out our hands to him

but he won't do anything for me living so long after his time and
surely he's fictional anyway so how can he help me get out of
this hanging about and hanging about for ever when I could be
doing something like going back and

walk haunt turn the room cold hear them talking and long for
someone to see me here I'm here my love can't you see me
hundreds of years still floating through walls I'm here I'm here
no I'm not a ghost story

going back and having another life my own life over again like
that movie and do it better of course because most of the time I
hardly noticed it going by and I used to look back and think
how careless I was when I was young I never noticed and by
then I was middle-aged and later I'd look back and think *then* I
never noticed

and another go would be welcome

but nobody suggests they do that in real life real death not
another go as yourself another go as somebody else or of course
some*thing* else

and have I lived the sort of life that would get me one step up to
be a happier better person one true love maybe I deserve to
paint or

no not be in power hate to be a president king general imagine
how terrible that might be a punishment of course a step down

or I might have to sleep in the street yes I'm walking miles with
a heavy sick child I'm so depressed I can't put on my socks

but I might not be human a bird a bird everyone wants to fly oh
a kestrel can I be a kestrel yes I can see every blade of grass and
a mouse drop on the mouse but I might be the mouse

I might be a rabid street dog foaming a cow up the ramp to the
slaughter

I'd rather be an endangered species some beautiful far far
anywhere oh

I might be an insect one of billions I am already one of billions
but trillions

a locust eating and eating do they feel joy do they just eat or
maybe a flea blood and the amazing jump

oh I don't want to be the caterpillar the wasp lays an egg in and
it hatches and consumes from inside

but surely that's not a belief I've ever I've never

and I wouldn't be me this one I've been doesn't remember
others it's extinction of me even if I'm part of some cosmic
whatsit drop gone back to the ocean no

and of course all the bits of my body are on their way now
breaking down into smaller and smaller rather disgusting at first
but into the daisies

or did they have me cremated how odd I don't know in which
case it's all gone up in smoke leaving just those gritty ashes that
might be partly someone else's I'm not sure how particular they
are at the crem when they sweep it out

but anyway all the chemicals atoms neutrons from stars on their
way because the energy's still all there

but not my energy like 'oh I'm so tired today I've got no energy'
now I've really got no energy it's somewhere else like before I
was born

all those atoms are somewhere else

and you're just a thing that happens like an elephant or a
daffodil

and there you all are for a short time

that's how it's put together for a short time

and oddly you are actually are one of those

and it goes on and on and you're used to it and then suddenly

3. GETTING THERE

A very old or ill person and a carer.

The old/ill person is in nightclothes and is helped by the carer to get dressed, slowly and with difficulty because of pain and restricted movement.

Then to get undressed and back into nightclothes.

Then to get dressed.

Then to get undressed and back into nightclothes.

Then to get dressed...

for as long as the scene lasts.

End.

ESCAPED ALONE

Escaped Alone was first performed at the Royal Court Theatre
Downstairs, London, on 21 January 2016. The cast was as
follows:

MRS JARRETT   Linda Bassett
SALLY   Deborah Findlay
LENA   Kika Markham
VI   June Watson

Director   James Macdonald
Designer   Miriam Buether
Lighting Designer Peter Mumford
Sound Designer   Christopher Shutt

'I only am escaped alone to tell thee.'

Book of Job. Moby Dick.

Characters

SALLY
VI
LENA
MRS JARRETT

They are all at least seventy.

Place

Sally's backyard.

Several unmatching chairs. Maybe one's a kitchen chair.

Time

Summer afternoon.

A number of afternoons but the action is continuous.

1.

MRS J   I'm walking down the street and there's a door in the fence open and inside are three women I've seen before.

VI   Don't look now but there's someone watching us.

LENA   Is it that woman?

SALLY   Is that you, Mrs Jarrett?

MRS J   So I go in.

SALLY   Rosie locked out in the rain

VI   forgot her key

SALLY   climbed over

LENA   lucky to have neighbours who

SALLY   such a high wall

VI   this is Rosie her granddaughter

MRS J   I've a son, Frank

VI   I've a son

MRS J   suffers from insomnia

VI   doesn't come very often. But Thomas

LENA   that's her nephew

SALLY   he'd knock up the shelves in no time

VI   a big table

SALLY   grain of the wood

VI   a table like that would last a lifetime

SALLY	an heirloom
LENA	except we all eat off our laps
MRS J	nothing like a table
LENA	I like a table
VI	all have each other's keys because there's no way round and anyway I couldn't climb
MRS J	unless you lose them
VI .	no I hang them all on a nail
SALLY	in a teapot
VI	teapot?
SALLY	Elsie puts them in and takes them out
LENA	down the floorboards
VI	only use bags in mugs
SALLY	holds your finger and then takes one step and down she goes.
LENA	Barney never out of his phone
VI	I'd have been the same
LENA	looking pale
VI	whole worlds in your pocket
LENA	little bit worried about Kevin and Mary, never hear an endearment
SALLY	but nobody ever knows
MRS J	you'd be surprised what goes on
LENA	twenty years in June
VI	we had to wear hats
SALLY	a pink one and I didn't
VI	so you gave it to Angela
SALLY	I'd forgotten Angela

LENA	shadows under her eyes
VI	ended up with a green one and it didn't suit you
LENA	I could never say a word of course.
VI	And Maisie, never so happy
LENA	that's her niece
SALLY	quantum
VI	I can't really follow
SALLY	I can't even add up
LENA	they don't add up any more
VI	particles and waves I can manage but after that
SALLY	always good at sums as a child, she'd say two big numbers
VI	and while we were carrying things in our head
LENA	I needed a pencil
SALLY	she'd say the answer and it was always right
MRS J	I could always make change quick with the shillings and pence
VI	we'd be the ones got it wrong
LENA	easier now it's decimal
SALLY	always right.
LENA	And Vera

MRS J   Four hundred thousand tons of rock paid for by
senior executives split off the hillside to smash
through the roofs, each fragment onto the
designated child's head. Villages were buried and
new communities of survivors underground
developed skills of feeding off the dead where
possible and communicating with taps and groans.
Instant celebrities rose on ropes to the light of
flashes. Time passed. Rats were eaten by those
who still had digestive systems, and mushrooms
were traded for urine. Babies were born and
quickly became blind. Some groups lost their
sexuality while others developed a new morality of
constant fucking with any proximate body. A
young woman crawling from one society to the
other became wedged, only her head reaching her
new companions. Stories of those above ground
were told and retold till there were myths of the
husband who cooked feasts, the wife who swam
the ocean, the gay lover who could fly, the child
who read minds, the talking dog. Prayers were said
to them and various sects developed with tolerance
and bitter hatred. Songs were sung until dry
throats caused the end of speech. Torrential rain
leaked through cracks and flooded the tunnels
enabling screams at last before drownings.
Survivors were now solitary and went insane at
different rates.

2.

SALLY	corner shop
LENA	don't like the
VI	mini Tesco
LENA	bit far
MRS J	used to be the fish and chip shop
VI	that other one's gone
SALLY	the old grocer
VI	I'd do a shop for seventeen shillings
LENA	so what's that in
MRS J	fifteen's seventyfive p
VI	but we earned nothing too
SALLY	so who does the shopping if you can't go out?
LENA	I do go
VI	is Kevin a help?
SALLY	I could always
VI	but it's good for you to go yourself
SALLY	good to get out
LENA	I do get out
SALLY	you're here
LENA	it's not easy
SALLY	antique shop now but in between it was that café
VI	it was never a café
SALLY	the Blue something, an animal

MRS J	I been there
SALLY	Hedgehog, something unlikely
VI	I don't think so
SALLY	maybe it was when
LENA	oh
SALLY	that would be it of course
VI	I did miss a few things when I was away
MRS J	away was you?
LENA	just a little while
VI	six years
SALLY	that's what it was then, Blue Antelope
VI	antique shops now but down the other end
SALLY	yes three shops boarded up
VI	that's the nail parlour and the old dentist
SALLY	did you ever go?
VI	he was terrible
SALLY	he was such a bad
VI	'this might just trouble you a little'
SALLY	oh my god
VI	half an hour to get there but so much better
LENA	I should go to the dentist
SALLY	a checkup
LENA	it must be five years
MRS J	you don't want toothache
LENA	it's just one more thing you have to do, one thing after another, I can't seem to
SALLY	I could always go with you

LENA	if I go
SALLY	or do some shopping
VI	it's good she gets out herself
LENA	I do get out
SALLY	and the chicken nuggets closed down
VI	that was the ironmongers
SALLY	no in between it was the health shop
LENA	a hammer and a spade
VI	there must be quite a few things I missed
SALLY	not really, it all goes by, I can't remember those years specially
VI	remember what was happening where I was of course
SALLY	yes of course
VI	though it gets to be a blur because it's all a bit the same
SALLY	it must have been
VI	unless there was an excitement like a fight
MRS J	fights was there?
VI	or love affairs
LENA	I do get out it's just difficult

MRS J   First the baths overflowed as water was
deliberately wasted in a campaign to punish the
thirsty. Swimming pools engulfed the leisure
centres and coffee ran down the table legs. Rivers
flowed back towards their tributaries and up the
streams to what had been trickles in moss. Ponies
climbed to high ground and huddled with the
tourists. Yawls, ketches, kayaks, canoes, schooners,
planks, dinghies, lifebelts and upturned umbrellas,
swimming instructors and lilos, rubber ducks and
pumice stone floated on the stock market. Waves
engulfed ferris wheels and drowned bodies were
piled up to block doors. Then the walls of water
came from the sea. Villages vanished and cities
relocated to their rooftops. Sometimes children fell
down the sewage chutes but others caught seagulls
with kites. Some died of thirst, some of drinking
the water. When the flood receded thousands
stayed on the roofs fed by helicopter while heroes
and bonded workers shovelled the muck into
buckets that were stored in the flood museums.

3.

VI	Parallel universes
SALLY	fiction
VI	scientists
SALLY	makes good stories
VI	second series
LENA	I'm watching the third
SALLY	does Elliott
MRS J	don't tell us
SALLY	too many universes for me
LENA	when I stay home I watch
VI	you've seen everything
SALLY	but you're feeling better
LENA	it just drops away, you wake up one morning and it's all right
SALLY	amazing
LENA	like a different world
VI	universe
MRS J	I don't like Elliott
VI	the way he looks at his wife
LENA	but you're meant to think that
SALLY	I do think that, I don't care
VI	and now the money
SALLY	Ursula's nasty

VI	I'm sorry for Ursula
SALLY	I think it's going to be Ursula
MRS J	four husbands
LENA	they want you to think that
VI	loved her in the first series
LENA	exactly
SALLY	but universes to get your mind round
LENA	the third series
VI	and the very very small
SALLY	yes our bodies
VI	millions of little creatures
LENA	makes my flesh creep
VI	fleas on a cat
LENA	microbes on a flea
VI	oh
LENA	oh
VI	sorry
LENA	look what you've done
MRS J	what's she done?
LENA	we don't mention
VI	are you all right?
MRS J	what, fleas?
VI	no
LENA	cats
VI	shh
LENA	are you all right?
SALLY	yes I'm fine thank you

VI   sorry I'm so sorry

SALLY   the third series

LENA   particles

VI   though mind you are we helping by never saying?

LENA   don't start that

SALLY   it's all right, you needn't

VI   shouldn't we just say it, say black and white, tabby, longhaired, shorthaired, siamese

MRS J   I've got a lovely tabby but he's a tom so

LENA   stop it

VI   expose her to it and nothing bad happens and she gets used to nothing bad

LENA   stop it

VI   I'm helping

MRS J   is she going to faint?

SALLY   no no I'm

LENA   see?

VI   I'm sorry I just get

SALLY   I know it's stupid

VI   no

SALLY   I know you hate me sometimes

VI   no, I

LENA   see?

SALLY   you just need to face

VI   I need to face?

SALLY   how unpleasant you can be

LENA   see?

VI   oh it's me now, it's always someone

LENA   stop it

MRS J   let's hear it

SALLY   it doesn't bother me

VI   oh let's not

SALLY   it's fine

VI   I know I shouldn't

SALLY   so tell us about the third series

MRS J   don't tell us about the third series

LENA   I'll just hint that Elliott

VI   don't say it

MRS J   The chemicals leaked through cracks in the
money. The first symptoms were irritability and
nausea. Domestic violence increased and there
were incidents on the underground. School
absenteeism tripled and ninetyseven schools were
taken into special measures. Dog owners cleared
up their pets' vomit or risked a fine. Miscarriages
were frequent leading to an increase of
opportunities in grief counselling. Birth
deformities outpaced the immigration of plastic
surgeons. Gas masks were available on the NHS
with a three month waiting time and privately in a
range of colours. Sometimes the cancers began in
the lungs and sometimes on the fingertips or
laptops. The remaining citizens were evacuated to
camps in northern Canada where they were
sprayed and victimised, and the city was left to sick
foxes, who soon abandoned it for lack of dustbins.

4.

LENA	So how many noughts
VI	a billion has nine
SALLY	no
VI	a trillion
SALLY	a billion has twelve
VI	no, we adopted the American
SALLY	are you saying a billion isn't a million million?
VI	a thousand million now, and a trillion
SALLY	oh I don't like that
MRS J	what's a zillion?
VI	and then of course you get a googol and a googolplex, which isn't the same as
LENA	a zillion's what you say, is it a real
VI	three Brazilians dead and President Bush said Oh no, remind me how many is a brazilian
SALLY	he's taken the place of moron
LENA	moron?
SALLY	when I was a child Little Moron jokes for anything stupid, what did the Little Moron say when he
VI	what did he say?
LENA	no one says moron
SALLY	they keep having to change what you can say because whatever word they use becomes
VI	did we ever say moron for jokes? is it American or

LENA	but you can't even make that kind of joke not about mentally
SALLY	Irish for a long time, Irish jokes
MRS J	'no blacks no dogs no Irish'
SALLY	I remember that
VI	and we weren't even that shocked
LENA	we do shock easier
VI	but you have to have jokes about stupid things someone might do because anyone might, it's funny
LENA	you can't have a class of people
SALLY	you could have yourself
VI	you could have me
SALLY	what did I say when I jumped off the top of
VI	don't the comedians do that, they make themselves
SALLY	but of course we know they're clever.
LENA	So in other countries do they have that?
VI	jokes about being stupid?
LENA	making out it's some neighbour who's
SALLY	you always get people hating their neighbours
VI	yes the closer they are
SALLY	Serbs and Croats, French and English
LENA	there's history though
SALLY	but anyone everyone outside thinks is the same
VI	Catholics and Protestants, Sunni and Shia
MRS J	Arsenal and Tottenham
SALLY	there you are
LENA	Cain and Abel

VI	did Abel make jokes about Cain being stupid and that's why he killed him?
LENA	odd they needed a story about how killing started because
SALLY	chimpanzees
LENA	but you do wonder why of course so you make a story
VI	easily done I found
SALLY	different each time
VI	I don't know why, I never knew why
MRS J	found it easy did you?
LENA	never mind that
SALLY	not always easy and a lot of men in the war never fired their guns because
VI	no it's all right, she can know
MRS J	what can I know?
VI	tell her, go on
LENA	she accidentally
SALLY	a long time ago
LENA	accidentally killed her husband
VI	not accidentally
LENA	in self defence
MRS J	how did you do that?
VI	kitchen knife happened to be in my hand
LENA	just bad luck really
VI	so when I hit back
MRS J	so that was all right was it, self defence
SALLY	more complicated

LENA	the lawyers
SALLY	manslaughter
VI	six years, which was half
MRS J	still a long time
VI	the first two years
LENA	things do speed up
SALLY	everything does
MRS J	you get used to it
SALLY	so that can be good but when it's your whole life speeding up
LENA	don't start on that
SALLY	I'd like to have time travel
VI	knock knock
LENA	who's there?
VI	Dr
SALLY	that's a six year old's joke.

MRS J   The hunger began when eighty per cent of food
         was diverted to tv programmes. Commuters
         watched breakfast on iPlayer on their way to work.
         Smartphones were distributed by charities when
         rice ran out, so the dying could watch cooking.
         The entire food stock of Newcastle was won by
         lottery ticket and the winner taken to a
         24 hour dining room where fifty chefs chopped in
         relays and the public voted on what he should eat
         next. Cars were traded for used meat. Children fell
         asleep in class and didn't wake up. The obese sold
         slices of themselves until hunger drove them to eat
         their own rashers. Finally the starving stormed the
         tv centres and were slaughtered and smoked in
         large numbers. Only when cooking shows were
         overtaken by sex with football teams did cream
         trickle back to the shops and rice was airlifted
         again.

5.

VI	People always want to fly
LENA	fly like a bird
SALLY	that's always the favourite, what would you like
LENA	invisible
VI	languages, I'd like to be able to speak every
SALLY	but we do fly now
MRS J	planes isn't the same
VI	go to any country at all and understand
SALLY	and nobody looks out of the window
LENA	watching the screens
VI	I do like getting all those movies I never
SALLY	looking down on clouds
LENA	yes what would Julius Caesar have thought or
SALLY	and they make it like being in a very unpleasant room
VI	try to make you forget you're up in the air
LENA	because it could be frightening being up in the air
SALLY	because that's not what people mean by flying
VI	flying like a bird in the sky
LENA	but if people could, if we all
VI	that's no good
LENA	imagine the crowds
SALLY	at rush hour
LENA	separate lanes

SALLY	flocks
VI	like starlings, that would be good, all those shapes
LENA	flocks of pigeons, they seem to change colour
SALLY	no we wouldn't have that sense of each other, we'd keep bumping
VI	but what people want is fly by yourself
LENA	straight up like a lark
VI	or hover like what?
LENA	a kestrel
VI	kestrel yes
LENA	or an eagle
VI	soar like an eagle
MRS J	I wouldn't want to be a pigeon
VI	we're not being birds we're us but able to
SALLY	pigeons are like rats
LENA	pigeons are not
VI	looking down from above
SALLY	like drones with cameras
LENA	Barney's got one, remote control, you can see as if you're
VI	I hate that because they bomb and they're not in danger
LENA	it's just a toy
SALLY	is it all right to bomb if you are in danger?
VI	but no it's not the seeing it's the sensation
LENA	soaring and diving
SALLY	like swimming under water really going up and down

VI   no only if you can scuba

LENA   hate putting my head under water

VI   birds is better than fish

MRS J   I wouldn't want to be a fish

LENA   or being invisible is the one I'd like

SALLY   all this about birds, I don't quite like about birds
            because birds leads to cats, pigeons leads to cats,
            cat among the pigeons, next door's tabby had a
            pigeon such flapping and couldn't kill it, wouldn't,
            just played about kept grabbing it again and the
            bird was maimed someone had to ugh, and
            pigeons like rats leads to cats rats cats rats are filthy
            plague everywhere, only how many feet from a rat,
            and pigeons are filthy, rats are filthy, cats are filthy
            their bites are poison they bite you and the bite
            festers, but that's not it that's not it I know that's
            just an excuse to give a reason I know I've no
            reason I know it's just cats cats themselves are the
            horror because they're cats and I have to keep
            them out I have to make sure I never think about a
            cat because if I do I have to make sure there's no
            cats and they could be anywhere they could get in
            a window I have to go round the house and make
            sure all the windows are locked and I don't know
            if I checked properly I can't remember I was too
            frightened to notice I have to go round the
            windows again I have to go round the windows
            again back to the kitchen back to the bedroom
            back to the kitchen back to the bedroom the
            bathroom back to the kitchen back to the door, the
            door might blow open if it's windy even if it's not
            windy suppose the postman was putting a large
            packet and pushed the door and it came open
            because it wasn't properly shut and then a cat
            because they can get through very very small and
            once they're in they could be anywhere they could
            be under the bed in the wardrobe up on the top
            shelf with the winter sweaters that would be a

place for a cat to sleep or in a wastepaper basket
or under the cushions on the sofa or in the
cupboard with the saucepans or in the cupboard
with the food a cat could curl up on the cans of
tomatoes a cat could be in with the jam and honey
a cat could be in the biscuit tin, a cat could be in
the fridge in the freezer in the salad drawer in the
box of cheese in the broom cupboard the mop
bucket a cat could be in the oven the top oven
under the lid of the casserole in a box of matches
behind a picture under a rug back to the bedroom
a cat could be under the bed in the duvet in the
pillowcase in the wardrobe a cat could be in a shoe
on a hanger under my dress in a woolly hat inside
a coat sleeve a cat could be in any of the drawers
so I tip them all out and shake every – cat behind
the books on the shelf behind the dvds a cat could
be in the teapot with the keys a cat could be on the
ceiling a cat could be on top of the door a cat
could be behind me a cat could be under my hand
when I put out my hand. I need someone to say
there's no cats, I need to say to someone do you
smell cat, I need to say do you think there's any
way a cat could have got in, and they have to say
of course not, they have to say of course not, I
have to believe them, it has to be someone I
believe, I have to believe they're not just saying it, I
have to believe they know there are no cats, I have
to believe there are no cats. And then briefly the
joy of that.

LENA	Eagles you get eagles as national
VI	eagles are fascist
LENA	America has the eagle
VI	well
MRS J	I wouldn't mind being an eagle
SALLY	very often fascist
LENA	shame for the eagle really, it little knows

VI	an eagle wouldn't have much empathy
SALLY	nor would a blackbird come to that
VI	you don't get blackbirds as national
LENA	do religions have birds?
VI	dove of peace
SALLY	sacred ibis
LENA	you could have bird rituals
SALLY	scattering of birdseed
VI	bird calls by the congregation
LENA	holy ghost of course that gets pictured sometimes as
SALLY	that's the dove of peace
VI	I thought the holy ghost was invisible
LENA	I'd rather be invisible myself.

MRS J   The wind developed by property developers
          started as breezes on cheeks and soon turned
          heads inside out. The army fired nets to catch
          flying cars but most spun by with dozens clinging
          and shrieking, dropping off slowly. Buildings
          migrated from London to Lahore, Kyoto to
          Kansas City, and survivors were interned for
          having no travel documents. Some in the
          whirlwind went higher and higher, the airsick
          families taking selfies in case they could ever share
          them. Shanty towns were cleared. Pets rained from
          the sky. A kitten became famous.

6.

All sing. **SALLY**, **VI** *and* **LENA** *in harmony.* **MRS JARRETT** *joins
in the melody. They are singing for themselves in the garden, not performing
to the audience.*

MRS J   The illness started when children drank sugar
          developed from monkeys. Hair fell out, feet
          swelled, organs atrophied. Hairs blowing in the
          wind rapidly passed round the world. When they
          fell into the ocean cod died and fishermen blew up
          each other's boats. Planes with sick passengers
          were diverted to Antarctica. Some got into bed
          with their dead, others locked the doors and ran
          till they fell down. Volunteers and conscripts over
          seven nursed the sick and collected bodies.
          Governments cleansed infected areas and made
          deals with allies to bomb each other's capitals.
          Presidents committed suicide. The last survivors
          had immunity and the virus mutated,
          exterminating plankton.

7.

SALLY	I miss work
VI	I don't miss work at all
SALLY	you're learning Spanish
VI	you're in love
SALLY	a little
MRS J	in love are you?
VI	your job was far
SALLY	could be very boring of course
VI	no all the people and all
SALLY	yes but endless colds coughs coughs sore throats coughs
VI	'antibiotics please'
SALLY	and of course you have to be alert
VI	because sometimes
SALLY	you don't want to miss cancer
VI	did you ever?
SALLY	terrible occasion
MRS J	I go to that Dr Meadows
SALLY	reliable though
MRS J	but you can't get an appointment
VI	envy you doing good
SALLY	made your clients happy
MRS J	what did you

VI	hairdresser
MRS J	cut my own hair, cut my husband's hair
SALLY	tell you their troubles
VI	they did
MRS J	didn't look very good mind
SALLY	and you didn't have to fix the troubles just fix the hair
VI	that's true
SALLY	while I was supposed to fix
VI	and you could sometimes
SALLY	sometimes I could
VI	because hair's a bit trivial
SALLY	yes but you can feel quite new with a different
VI	or miserable if you don't like it
SALLY	the first day or two
VI	kept coming back every couple of days
SALLY	shorter and shorter?
VI	shorter, different colours, I finally had to
MRS J	the hair wasn't the problem
VI	it wasn't the problem
SALLY	and you really don't miss it
VI	I do now we're talking about
SALLY	though I do enjoy the days
VI	yes having the afternoons
MRS J	when I was a lollipop lady a few years back
SALLY	that's afternoon work of course and morning and lunchtime

MRS J   give it up after a month

LENA   I couldn't keep on

VI   you loved that office

LENA   I did

VI   such a highflying

LENA   some days it would be all right for weeks but then
          I'd find it coming down again. You're so far away
          from people at the next desk. Email was better
          than speaking. It's down now.
          Why can't I just?
          I just can't.
          I sat on the bed this morning and didn't stand up
          till lunchtime. The air was too thick. It's hard to
          move, it's hard to see why you'd move.
          It's not so bad in the afternoon, I got myself here.
          I don't like it here. I've no interest.
          Why talk about that? Why move your mouth and
          do talking? Why see anyone? Why know about
          anyone?
          It was half past three and all this time later it's
          twentyfive to four.
          If I think about a place I could be where there's
          something nice like the sea that would be worse
          because the sea would be the same as an empty
          room so it's better to be in the empty room
          because then there's fewer things to mean nothing
          at all.
          I'd rather hear something bad than something
          good. I'd rather hear nothing.
          It's still just the same.
          It's just the same.
          It's the same.

SALLY   Your medication doesn't seem very

VI   do you take it?

LENA   it's not an easy thing to

SALLY   not a sprained ankle

MRS J	I had my hips done
VI	and is that
MRS J	two new hips I can walk all day
SALLY	my knee
VI	my back doing hair on my feet all day
SALLY	yes at least I sat
VI	exactly
SALLY	but then I ran
VI	I missed it when I had to stop
MRS J	was that when you was
VI	six years
MRS J	did you go back to hair after?
VI	not the same place, it was never such a good
SALLY	you did several different
VI	out of work completely a long time
MRS J	not fair because it was just self defence was it
VI	it was
LENA	not fair really
SALLY	more complicated
LENA	self defence
SALLY	fair enough really
LENA	you think?
SALLY	because if I'd said
LENA	said what?
SALLY	said what happened
LENA	what happened?
SALLY	it was complicated

MRS J   you was there was you?

SALLY   in the kitchen

VI   you'd had a drink of course

SALLY   we all had, that's why

VI   are you saying

SALLY   I'm just saying I didn't quite

VI   what? come on what? are you saying

SALLY   I didn't tell it quite how it was because

VI   you did

SALLY   no because I took into account what he was like

LENA   it wasn't murder

SALLY   could have been that's all I'm saying if I hadn't

VI   if you hadn't what?

SALLY   hadn't said it in a way that worked out

MRS J   lied in the witness box did you?

SALLY   she's my friend, of course I

VI   you thought you were lying

SALLY   I thought I was economical

VI   you think I murdered him?

SALLY   it's not a matter really of defining

VI   you think I'm a murderer?

SALLY   it doesn't really

VI   all this time you've thought

SALLY   it was so long ago

VI   you think

SALLY   I don't care if you are

VI   I care

SALLY   so long ago

VI   you think

SALLY   look I'm sorry

VI   no what

SALLY   sorry, I shouldn't have

VI   what

SALLY   I don't know what I mean even

LENA   what did you say?

SALLY   I don't even know what I said any more

MRS J   what did you see?

SALLY   certainly don't know what I saw any more

VI   you think I'm a murderer

SALLY   maybe you were I don't know do you think you're a murderer

VI   no

SALLY   okay so maybe you weren't

VI   I don't remember either

MRS J   you don't remember what you

VI   no it's gone

SALLY   there you are then.

VI   I missed cutting hair and I missed food

LENA   prison food

VI   not that I'm much of a cook

MRS J   Frank can cook

VI   I missed snacks in prison and I missed apples

MRS J   Fire broke out in ten places at once. Four cases of arson by children and politicians, three of spontaneous combustion of the markets, two of sunshine, one supposed by believers to be a punishment by God for gender dysphoria. It swept through saplings, petrol stations, prisons, dryads and books. Fires were lit to stop the fires and consumed squirrels, firefighters and shoppers. Cars sped from one furnace to another. Houses exploded. Some shot flaming swans, some shot their children. Finally the wind drove the fire to the ocean, where salt water made survivors faint. The blackened area was declared a separate country with zero population, zero growth and zero politics. Charred stumps were salvaged for art and biscuits.

8.

VI	Thomas finished the table
SALLY	love to see it
VI	sit round it before it goes
LENA	bought by some rich
VI	not rich rich not as if it was art
SALLY	art's ridiculous
VI	they buy it just so they can sell it they don't even look
SALLY	Rosie paints very
VI	just for yourself
LENA	and photographs I've always liked
SALLY	easy with phones
LENA	pictures of seabirds, gannets
MRS J	what's gannets?
VI	black, hold their wings out
LENA	that's cormorants
VI	puffins are the ones with beaks, I've never seen
SALLY	you'd have to go somewhere with rocks
LENA	gannets are big and white
MRS J	like a gull
LENA	bigger
SALLY	not like an albatross
VI	albatross round your neck

LENA	fly for years and years and never land.
VI	Birds can be frightening
SALLY	birds?
VI	if they swoop down
MRS J	no that's bats, they get in your hair
SALLY	they don't really
LENA	I was told as a child
SALLY	bats are worse because they zigzag
VI	'bat bat come under my hat, I'll give you a slice of bacon'
LENA	what's that?
VI	I don't know, I just know it
LENA	you'd hardly want it under your hat if you don't even like birds.
SALLY	Elsie chases birds
LENA	Elsie the dog?
VI	Elsie the dog's been dead five years
SALLY	Elsie the baby.
LENA	Dinner with Kevin and Mary
SALLY	did you get an impression
LENA	very cheerful, delicious lamb
SALLY	enjoy cooking sometimes
MRS J	Frank likes a lamb chop
LENA	I do love a kitchen
SALLY	my grandmother's kitchen
LENA	mine's more of a cupboard
SALLY	mine needs a coat of paint

LENA   would Rosie do it?

SALLY   do it myself, just need to make time

MRS J   I can't go up a ladder

LENA   that same dark orange or maybe

VI   I can't love a kitchen, I can't love a kitchen any
            more, if you've killed someone in a kitchen you're
            not going to love that kitchen, I lost that flat, even
            the kitchen where I am now reminds me of that
            kitchen, completely different colour, the cooker's
            on the other wall, and the window, but maybe it's
            the smell of food cooking, it's meat does it,
            cooking meat, the blood if it's rare, we don't often
            have meat, when you've cut somebody and seen
            the blood you don't feel the same, when he fell
            down you think oh good oh good and then you
            think that's a mistake, take that back, the horror
            happens then, keep that out, the horror is the
            whole thing is never the same, he's never a person
            alive somewhere any more, never the same with
            my son is the worst thing never forgive me how do
            you talk to a twelve year old when you've killed his
            father you can't explain everything the whole
            marriage what it's been like you don't want to
            make him hate his father you do want to make
            him hate his father but it wouldn't be right you
            don't want him to think you're someone who
            would try to make him hate his father, he was
            twelve, he'd visit me, it's hard to talk to a teenager
            if you're not seeing him all the time you need to
            be saying things like tidy your room have you done
            your homework do you want to watch a movie, I
            thought he'd be completely grown up but I got
            time off you have to do good behaviour, six years
            he was eighteen he was grown up he was living by
            himself he'd moved up north he's got a life I'm
            glad he's got a life, he's got a new partner again he
            phones sometimes, at least he phones, that's the
            worst thing even worse than the blood and the

thrashing about and what went wrong that's a horror but the horror goes on not seeing him he's got a life, it comes over me sometimes in the kitchen or in the night if I wake up sometimes if it's hot that's worse I can't breathe properly it all comes back in the night, but you get up in the morning and that's better put the kettle on but it's always there not there in the kitchen it's always there.

LENA   Maisie's a good cook

VI   I'm lucky with Maisie

SALLY   all those nieces

VI   I'm lucky with all those

LENA   Maisie bakes

VI   yes but not crazy baking

LENA   a nice sponge

VI   she'd do a birthday cake for her sisters.

SALLY   Rosie's going to China

VI   Rosie?

LENA   holiday or?

SALLY   university

VI   will she learn Mandarin?

LENA   always wanted to go to Japan

SALLY   get to Tesco first

VI   that's nasty

SALLY   no

VI   yes

SALLY   joke

VI   ha

LENA   I thought it was funny.

MRS J   Terrible rage terrible rage terrible rage terrible
              rage terrible rage terrible rage terrible rage terrible
              rage terrible rage terrible rage terrible rage terrible
              rage terrible rage terrible rage terrible rage terrible
              rage terrible rage terrible rage terrible rage terrible
              rage terrible rage terrible rage terrible rage terrible
              rage terrible rage

VI   Why did the chicken not cross the road?

SALLY   why did the chicken not cross the road?

VI   a car was coming

SALLY   that's just silly.

LENA   The sun's gone

VI   this time of day

SALLY   this time of year the shadow comes up earlier

LENA   still it's nice

VI   always nice to be here

MRS J   I like it here

SALLY   afternoons like this.

MRS J   And then I said thanks for the tea and I went
              home.

              End.

PIGS AND DOGS

Pigs and Dogs was first performed at the Royal Court Theatre Downstairs, London, on 20 July 2016. The cast was as follows:

Fisayo Akinade
Sharon D Clarke
Alex Hassell

Director	Dominic Cooke
Lighting Designer	Jack Williams
Sound Designer	David McSeveney

Note

Three actors, any gender or race but not all the same. Each can play any character, regardless of the character's race or gender.

A dash – means a new speaker.

The play is substantially based on material from *Boy-Wives and Female Husbands* by Stephen O. Murray and Will Roscoe.

– Somebody says

– President of Gambia

– We will fight these vermins
the way we fight malaria-bearing mosquitoes.

– Somebody says

– President Mugabe

– If dogs and pigs don't do it
why must human beings?

– Somebody posts

– You western-backed goats.
They forced us into slavery and killed millions.
Now they want to downplay the sinfulness of homo.
It shall not work.

– Somebody says

– Zuma, South Africa

– When I was growing up an ungqingili
would not have stood before me.
I would knock him out.

– Uganda.
Anti Homosexuality Act 2014.
Death penalty.
Later amended
to life imprisonment.

−   I know I shouldn't have sent him to that white
      school.

−   Somebody says

−   Ethics Minister in Uganda

−   If I kissed a man
      I think I should die, I could not exist.
      It is inhuman.
      Just imagine
      Eating your own faeces.

−   Newspaper says

−   Two hundred top homosexuals.

−   Names, pictures.

−   Hang them.

−   Museveni says

−   President of Uganda

−   Ugandan independence in the face of western
      pressure.

−   Mugabe says

−   President of Zimbabwe

−   We have our own culture.

−   Somebody says

−   in America

−   member of a rap group

–   There is no word in any African language that
describes homosexual.

–   But

–   sagoda never marry and wear skirts

–   ashtime dress like women and do women's work

–   mumenke is a man-woman

–   wasagu is a lesbian

–   yan daudu

–   umukonotsi

–   m'zili

–   tongo

–   kitesha

–   chibadi

–   ovashangi

–   wobo

–   If I had been a man
I could have taken a wife and begat children.

      If I had been a woman
I could have taken a husband and borne children.
But I am neither. I am wobo.

–   Somebody says

–   American intellectual

–   Homosexuality
is not always a conceptual category.

–   Hausa, yan daudu

–   Yes, I'm yan daudu, we dress like women,
we sing and dance and serve the fried chicken.
We can still get married and give a girl children.
You don't have to love her to give a girl children.

–   Hausa

–   Kwazo means work and that's male.
Baja means goods and that's female.

–   Two men can be kwazo and baja.

–   An old woman can be kwazo and her young
    husband is the baja
because she has the power.

–   Two women together is kifi
when the two have equal power.
Two men together can be kifi
if they both have equal power.

–   It's play, wasa, play.

–   You want someone and it's iskanci,

–   craziness.

–   Somebody says

–   Evans-Pritchard, anthropologist, last century

–   My informant Kuagbiaru says

–   this is how it used to be with the Zande.

–   The boy's my wife.
I asked for his hand with five spears
the same way you ask for a maiden.
That man who had sex with him must pay me
    compensation.
Soon he'll choose his own boy-wife like all the
    warriors,

I'll find another one.
When a prince dies his boys are killed so no one else
   can have them.

–   A king of the Maale in Ethiopia

–   a long time ago

–   the king could say

–   Because I'm king I'm the most male man.
   Everyone below me is less and less
   and least male of all is the ashtime.
   The night before a ritual I must abstain from
      women.
   I'm happy with my ashtime.

–   Nzinga of Ndongo

–   seventeenth century

–   succeeded her brother.

–   I am the king, I dress as a man.
   I have a harem of men dressed as women.
   I raised an army to fight the Portuguese
   and kept Ndongo free for forty years.

–   Mujaji the first
   queen of the Lovedu

–   this is Lesotho, nineteenth century

–   I have a harem
   they are all young women.
   I am helped to rule
   by mothers of the kingdom.
   There are many queens
   among Bantu people.

–   Women in Dahomey

–   eighteenth century

–   soldiers.

–   We never get married, we live like men.
     Prostitutes are kept for us like for the men.

–   We marched against the Attahpahms as if they were
          men
     but we found them women
     and defeated them.

–   We are no longer women.
     We are men.

–   The Fon in Dahomey

–   When we stop being small
     we're kept from the girls
     so we turn to each other.

–   Most of us grow up to take women for wives.

–   But we've stayed together
     all our lives.

–   And a woman in Ghana

–   This is not so long ago

–   We girls had each other,
     now we're married.
     We buy big beds
     and still meet each other.

–   Again in Ghana

–   Man or woman,
     if you have a heavy soul

you desire a woman.
Man or woman,
if you have a light soul
you desire a man.

–   Somebody says

–   Nuer in Ethiopia

–   Men here don't have sex with men.
It's different with that man because he's a woman.
It was decided by a prophet of Denge
and now she can take a husband like a woman.

–   In Lesotho
a woman says

–   I chose this woman as my friend.
We have two feasts with both our husbands,
killing sheep and dancing and singing,
gifts and guests, just like a wedding.

–   A woman of ninetyseven says

–   Haven't you ever fallen in love with another girl?

–   In Lesotho
a woman says

–   In Lesotho
women like to kiss each other.
And it's nothing. Except sometimes.

–   Somebody says in Burkina Faso

–   Gender is not the same as anatomy.
The earth is very delicate machinery
with high vibration points,
and some people must be the guardians
to keep the continuity
with the spirits of this world and the other.

The one who binds the spirits is the gatekeeper.
His vibrational consciousness is far higher
and that makes him gay.
You don't get chosen,
you choose it yourself before you're born.
You come into the world with that vibration
and the Elders know you're connected to
    a gateway.

–   English law.

–   English law says 1533

–   Forasmuch as there is not yet sufficient
and condign punishment
for the detestable and abominable
vice of buggery,
it may please the King's Highness
with the assent of the Lords Spiritual
and the Commons of this present Parliament
that the same offence be henceforth judged a felony.

–   Hang them.

–   Somebody says

–   Englishman in Angola
sixteenth century

–   They are beastly in their living
for they have men in women's apparel
whom they keep among their wives.

–   A missionary says

–   Seventeenth century

–   Sodomy is rampant in the south of Angola.

–   Missionaries, missionaries

–   Unnatural damnation

–   Detestable vices

–   Forsaking the natural use of women

–   Copulation contre nature.

–   Seventeenth century

–   Father Cavazzi

–   in the Congo as a missionary.

–   The Ganga-ya-Chibanda
is the most powerful Ganga.
He dresses like a woman
and is called the Grandmother.
He dresses
for sacrifices
in the skin
of a lion.
He has bells to call the gods of peace
and spirits of the dead.
He kills a snake,
a dog and a cock,
they bury the dog's head.
And the spirits show him where to find it.
Of course it's a trick,
he's told where to find it.
When he dies
he's buried in the forest
with such indecent ceremonies
the page would blush, so I can't write it.
They pull out his heart and liver
and hack off his toes and fingers
and sell them as relics.
And the colonial governor
can do nothing at all without the help of the Ganga.

–   Father Cavazzi writes

–   This information is for the missionaries
consecrated to the people's instruction.
Somewhat fruitless up to now.

–   Somebody says

–   Italian explorer 1900

–   Men in Eritrea
sleep with little devils.
No one thinks it's evil.
Diavoletti.

–   Somebody says

–   German anthropologist 1923

–   Homosexual intercourse
from Orange to the Congo.
It's generally widespread.

–   The laws against sodomy
were imported to the colonies.
Repealed in Britain
but thriving in the colonies.
Thriving in the countries
that used to be colonies.

–   We try them in the courts.

–   They had connection

–   fundamental orifice

–   obtained his purpose.

–   I was only playing.

–   Beating your wife

–   (She ends up dead)

–   Three months in prison.

Emitting semen on another man's legs
Six months in prison.

–   Somebody says

–   Ovambo chief

–   I know it is forbidden.
I shoot them with my Browning.

–   Museveni says

–   President of Uganda. 2014

–   This Act that we have passed
shows our independence
independence in the face of western pressure.

–   We have our own culture.

–   We will fight these vermins.

–   They are beasts of the forest

–   Mad people and criminals

–   Hand them over to the police

–   You cannot have a right to be a sick human being

–   Homosexuality will destroy humanity because
there's no procreation

–   There is no right in homosexuality

–   It is sub-animal behaviour, we will not allow it

–   If they don't like it they can leave

–   It is unAfrican because it is inconsistent with African
values of procreation and belief in the clan

—   It is unnatural behaviour and strange to our culture.

—   Somebody says

—   Winnie Mandela

—   It is alien to our culture. It is filth.

—   Somebody says

—   American evangelists

—   We're losing America.

—   We're winning in Africa.

—   American evangelist

—   Gays are the agents
      of America's moral decline.
      The force behind Nazi atrocities.
      If they could get away with killing
      anyone opposed to them like yours truly,
      they'd do it.
      They have the media, academia, Hollywood,
         big corporations,
      mental health associations,
      even the US military.
      Uganda can be a country led by God.

—   American evangelist goes to Kampala, says

—   Homosexuals have a hidden and dark agenda.
      Evil.
      They threaten the marriage based society.

—   Ugandan legislator says
      at a Family Breakfast

–   (this is a secret Christian organisation,
        American organisation)

–   Let's consider execution.

–   American evangelist says

–   We're not involved in US politics
        much less in the politics of another nation.
        I don't support the death penalty
        but I support the Bill.
        I support the stand against evil.
        Winning in Africa.

–   We have our own culture.

–   Somebody says, somebody says

–   Either is equally good and beautiful.

–   I didn't know it was a crime.

–   Dogs do it, giraffes do it, flamingoes

–   If I wanted to have a woman I can get plenty.

–   I never noticed anything peculiar, he worked as
            a nurse, I thought him sound in his mind.

–   Why should we worry since we can't get pregnant?

–   Just staying together nicely.

–   People now don't love like they did long ago.

–   I was welcomed by his family.

–   We loved them better.

–   Somebody says

–   a Khoikhoi man

–   I wanted him so I gave him a cup of Sore-water.
Nice when it's coffee but water will do.
I said Sore-gansa-are!
Drink the Sore-water!
And he took it in his hands and drank it
which means Yes.

–   It's wasa, play.

–   It's iskanci, craziness.

–   Sometimes for all our lives.

WAR AND PEACE GAZA PIECE

War and Peace Gaza Piece was first read at the launch event of
a project called *War and Peace: Gaza (Palestine) – London (UK)
Tolstoy's novel as theatre* at Rich Mix, London, on
14 September 2014. The project was part of the ten-year
partnership (2009–2019) between Az Theatre (London) and
Theatre for Everybody (Gaza) called *Gaza Drama Long Term*. The
cast was as follows:

NARRATOR	Harriet Walter
MARIA	Anna Capper
FATHER	David Calder
LISA	Elsa Mullien
PIERRE	Joe Kloska
BABY	Tom Clark
Director	Jonathan Chadwick

NARRATOR	Maria Bolkonskaya is a young Russian girl and she is doing mathematics. Her father, the Old Prince, likes to watch.
MARIA	If the angle ABC is ninety degrees then the square on AC is equal to the sum of the squares on AB and BC.
FATHER	Can you prove it?
MARIA	Yes but I didn't figure it out myself, it's Pythagoras, don't you remember how to prove it?
FATHER	I'm not sure I do, can you show me?
NARRATOR	Lisa Bolkonskaya, his daughter-in-law, is sitting by the window.
LISA	What are my friends doing now in St Petersburg? Andrei loves his father and sister of course and I was glad to see them the first day but it goes on and on and this should be a specially nice time for me because I'm going to have a baby. What's Andrei doing now? Is the war really happening? Is he in a battle? What is that, really, a battle, what happens in it, how do they do it? Nobody tells me.
NARRATOR	Andrei's looking forward to a battle. He's having a drink tonight with his friend Pierre. He leaves in the morning.
ANDREI	A glorious war.
PIERRE	I don't know what you get out of it.
ANDREI	I'll be fighting Napoleon. What do you get out of peace?

NARRATOR   And Maria says

MARIA   The angles – what's that noise?

FATHER   Just thunder, let's close the window.

MARIA   It's getting nearer.

NARRATOR   And Lisa says

LISA   I've a stomach ache. I wonder if I ate something. It's better now. No, it's not. Oh, I wonder.

NARRATOR   And Andrei says

ANDREI   War's very loud.

NARRATOR   And Pierre says

PIERRE   Freedom.

NARRATOR   And Maria says

MARIA   I can't concentrate.

FATHER   Just start again and pay attention.

MARIA   I can't with all the noise. I'm frightened.

NARRATOR   And Lisa says

LISA   It hurts. I'm frightened. I want Andrei.

NARRATOR   And Andrei says

ANDREI   They just keep bombing.

NARRATOR   And Pierre says

PIERRE   What's happening?

NARRATOR   And Maria says

MARIA   I can't study any more.

FATHER   Don't sleep by the window, let's move your bed.

NARRATOR   And Lisa says

LISA	Why are they bombing while I'm having a baby?
NARRATOR	And Maria says
MARIA	Hold my hand.
NARRATOR	And the Old Prince says
FATHER	The baby's alive.
NARRATOR	And Andrei says
ANDREI	I'm lying on the ground looking at the sky.
NARRATOR	And Maria says
MARIA	Lisa's baby's alive but did you see them next door carrying their baby out?
NARRATOR	And the Old Prince says
FATHER	Andrei's disappeared. Nobody knows where he is. They haven't found his body.
NARRATOR	And Pierre says
PIERRE	Is there no news of Andrei?
NARRATOR	And Maria says
MARIA	Father.
NARRATOR	And the Old Prince says
FATHER	My palace is in ruins. There's nothing but rubble further than I can walk.
NARRATOR	And Lisa says
LISA	I never saw the baby.
NARRATOR	And Maria says
MARIA	I've no books any more.
NARRATOR	And Andrei says
ANDREI	Do you think I'll walk again?

NARRATOR   And the baby says

BABY   Will I live to be six? Will I live to be eighty-
             two? Will I play on the beach? Will my
             children play on the beach? Will Aunt Maria
             teach me mathematics? Will I go to the other
             countries that must be out there somewhere?
             Will I have quiet days where I cook dinner
             and laugh and get annoyed about some small
             thing I'll have forgotten tomorrow? Will I
             want to kill someone?

NARRATOR   And Pierre is at his estate and he's running
             through the forest and he falls over and he can
             smell pine needles and feel them pricking his
             cheek and he says

PIERRE   What can we do? What can we do?

TICKETS ARE NOW ON SALE

Tickets are Now On Sale was first performed as part of *Walking the Tightrope: the tension between art and politics*, produced by Offstage Theatre in association with Theatre Uncut, at Theatre Delicatessen, London, on 26 January 2015. The cast was as follows:

1	Naomi Ackie
2	Syrus Lowe

Director   Cressida Brown

Note

The actors should perform each scene as if they were repeating
the first scene with exactly the same intonations and actions.
They should pay no attention to the meaning of the different
words that have been substituted. It is the same scene repeated
three times, invaded by sponsorship.

1.

1 Is something the matter?

2 No, not at all.

1 Did you have a good day?

2 Yes, great.

1 Nice and sunny.

2 Yes, I had a sandwich in the park. Nice and sunny.

1 I do think there's something you're not telling me.

2 I'm really completely fine.

1 Good.

2 Ok then.

Pause.

1 I just think there's something you're not saying.

2 It's difficult.

1 So there is something?

2 It's nothing really.

1 What are you frightened of?

Pause.

 Why don't we go for a walk? It's still sunny.

2 Ok, let's go for a walk.

1 Good.

2 Good.

1 And then you'll tell me what's wrong.

2.

1   Is something the matter?

2   No, not at all.

1   Did you have a good bank?

2   Yes, Coutts.

1   Barclays and sunny.

2   Yes, I had oil in the park. Nice and BP.

1   I do think high-profile corporate partnership.

2   I'm really completely cutting-edge culture.

1   Good.

2   Shell then.

Pause.

1   I just think there's positive associations with our brand.

2   It's philanthropy.

1   So it is excellence and vision?

2   It's a mutually beneficial relationship really.

1   What are you frightened of?

Pause.

Why don't we experience the best of opera and ballet? It's still sunny.

2   Ok, let's maximise assets and nurture talent.

1   Good.

2   Good.

1   And then you'll position your logo.

3.

1 Is something the matter?

2 No, not Israel.

1 Did you have a good image?

2 Yes, vibrant.

1 Nice and positive.

2 Yes, I had a profound rebranding in the park. Culture and sunny.

1 I do think culture is a propaganda tool of the first rank.

2 I'm really completely style-section item.

1 Good.

2 Ok then.

Pause.

1 I just think show Israel's prettier face.

2 Film festival.

1 So this is cultural and scientific activity?

2 Art exhibition, falafel, really.

1 What are you frightened of?

Pause.

 Why don't we be energetic and colourful? It's still sunny.

2 Yes, let's attain high exposure abroad.

1 Good.

2 Good.

1 And then you'll celebrate Israel.

4.

1   Is something the matter?

2   Tar sands.

1   Did you have a good war?

2   Yes, massacre.

1   Bankers and crash.

2   Yes, I had financial misconduct in the park. Investment in arms trade.

1   I do think there's Israel's illegal occupation you're not telling me.

2   I'm really completely human-rights violations.

1   Gaza.

2   Ok then.

Pause.

1   I do think rising sea levels you're not saying.

2   It's carbon emissions.

1   So there is war crime?

2   It's whitewash greenwash really.

1   What are you frightened of?

Pause.

      Why don't we go for a perfect sponsorship opportunity? It's still money.

2   Yes, let's boost the brand image.

1   Good.

2   Good.

1   And then you'll tell me what's wrong.

End.

BEAUTIFUL EYES

Beautiful Eyes was first performed as part of *Top Trumps* at Theatre503, London, on 19 January 2017. The cast was as follows:

MOTHER   Michele Austin
SON   Laurence Ubong Williams
DAUGHTER   Yvette Boakye

Director   Cressida Brown

Characters

MOTHER
SON
YOUNGER SISTER

Not American, unless performed in America.

MOTHER   I don't want to meet her.

SON   Mum.

MOTHER   Of course I'll meet her. But I don't know how anyone could do that.

SON   You can't help it.

MOTHER   Can't help voting…?

SON   Oh I meant falling in love. I couldn't help it.

MOTHER   Well, that was before you knew I expect.

SON   There's other things to do than talk about politics.

MOTHER   But she must have shown the kind of person.

SON   She's a free spirit.

MOTHER   There's going to be war with China. There's going to be race riots. There's going to be rapes, there's going to be shooting. There's going to be happy oil companies and fire and floods and anyone south of the Tropic of Cancer is going to have to come north or die and in your lifetime.

SON   There's not going to be war with China. Listen.

MOTHER   Oh god I'm so angry.

SON   Listen, there's so many things you'll like about her. There's so many things you have in common. She goes camping, she likes walking, we could have that sort of holiday together. She likes wild swimming. She likes cats. She makes pancakes. She loves family, she'd do anything for her brother, she's so clever with presents. She helps her neighbours, she went and cooked dinner for an old lady next door who'd had a fall, just like you and Mrs Whatsit. She wants what's good for people. She works hard, everything she has she's earned, that's like you, her dad lost his job, she hates corruption. She and her friends are always short of money and then you see people with everything and how did they deserve it, yes? It makes you frantic that whatever you do you can't seem to fix things because the government never does, and big companies behind the scenes so you can't get at them, and that's her, she hates feeling helpless. She thinks America should stay home, she'd have been with you on that Iraq march if it was happening now. She says it's like there's a ruling class and she wants to bring it down because democracy means by the people. Her heart lifts up at big ideas. She's good.

MOTHER   And the pussy and the Mexicans? And the lies?

SON   There's always things you have to overlook when you vote. She went more with the feeling. She has her finger on the pulse, it's a time of change. You like change.

MOTHER   I like the kind of change I like.

SON   Be nice to her.

MOTHER   One good thing, I suppose it won't last.

SON   He'll be gone in four years. Some people think he'll get bored before that.

MOTHER   No, I mean you and her.

SON   Oh I see.

MOTHER   Even if he left he's got those awful people in all the jobs.

SON   The thing is we're going to get married.

YOUNGER SISTER *comes in.*

SISTER   What's happening?

MOTHER   He's going to marry someone who voted for Trump.

SISTER   You're going to get married?

MOTHER   He's going to give me grandchildren who are racists.

SISTER   Give me a hug. I don't believe in marriage but hey.

MOTHER   She voted for Trump.

SISTER   I don't know why you're so obsessed. Most people in the world don't even care. People are hungry anyway. They're angry already. America goes on being a bad guy so what? I'm late now, tell me about her tonight.

YOUNGER SISTER *goes.*

MOTHER   There's always divorce.

SON   Mum.

MOTHER   I suppose I will try to be nice to her. I won't hide what I think.

SON   Of course not. Thank you.

MOTHER   Fuck.

SON   She has beautiful eyes.

MOTHER   Fuck.

SON   The one you really don't want to meet is her brother.

End.

www.nickhernbooks.co.uk

facebook.com/nickhernbooks

twitter.com/nickhernbooks